Emily and Anne Brontë

THE PROFILES IN LITERATURE SERIES

GENERAL EDITOR: B. C. SOUTHAM, M.A. B.LITT. (OXON.)
Formerly Department of English, Westfield College, University of London

Volumes in the series include

Emily and Anne Brontë

by W. H. Stevenson
Senior Lecturer in English
University of Ibadan, Nigeria

LONDON
ROUTLEDGE & KEGAN PAUL
NEW YORK : HUMANITIES PRESS

First published 1968
by Routledge & Kegan Paul Ltd
Broadway House, 68–74 Carter Lane
London, E.C.4

Printed in Great Britain
by Northumberland Press Limited
Gateshead

SBN 7100 6224 9 (C)
SBN 7100 6234 6 (P)

The Profiles in Literature Series

This series is designed to provide the student of literature and the general reader with a brief and helpful introduction to the major novelists and prose writers in English, American and foreign literature.

Each volume will provide an account of an individual author's writing career and works, through a series of carefully chosen extracts illustrating the major aspects of the author's art. These extracts are accompanied by commentary and analysis, drawing attention to particular features of the style and treatment. There is no pretence, of course, that a study of extracts can give a sense of the works as a whole, but this selective approach enables the reader to focus his attention upon specific features, and to be informed in his approach by experienced critics and scholars who are contributing to the series.

The volumes will provide a particularly helpful and practical form of introduction to writers whose works are extensive or which present special problems for the modern reader, who can then proceed with a sense of his bearings and an informed eye for the writer's art.

An important feature of these books is the extensive reference list of the author's works and the descriptive list of the most useful biographies, commentaries and critical studies.

B.C.S.

Contents

CONTENTS

Emily and Anne Brontë—their life and work

The Brontë family

There were four surviving children in the Brontë family;
Charlotte (born 1816), Branwell, the only boy (born 1817),
Emily Jane (born 1818) and Anne (born 1820). Their father,
Patrick, was a clergyman in the rural area between
Bradford and Keighley in the West Riding of Yorkshire,
first at Thornton and then at Haworth. (Keighley is pronounced 'Keethley'; the first syllable of Haworth has a
'short' vowel, as in had.) This is an area of high moorland,
grass and heather and open fields, on the ridge of the
Pennines, the land used as best it can be—mixed farming,
with corn and cattle on the better land, sheep on the high
pastures and open moor. During this generation the nearby
valleys of this part of the West Riding were going through
the throes of the rapid industrialisation of the textile
industry. There was growing wealth and prosperity side by
side with poverty, disease and injustice: but there is little
in the novels of the three sisters to show this.

The children were brought up by an aunt after their
mother's death in 1821. The family's life was socially
circumscribed by Mr. Brontë's vocation; a parson's circle
of acquaintances was small, and the West Riding was not

the country of Jane Austen's novels, with a wide range of 'gentry' for him to mix with. The children had to find most of their entertainment for themselves. Their father had published some writings—prose and verse fiction; the family subscribed to a circulating library. It is not surprising that the children, driven in on themselves, should turn to the pleasures of imagination, and to writing. In their teens, when most people begin to edge their way out from the home to independence in a wider society, they were already writing fiction—making a world of their own into which they turned the flow of their imaginative life. They invented in a play the 'Glasstown Confederacy', and then together wrote romantic tales about it. Later they divided; Charlotte and Branwell wrote about *Angria*, and Emily and Anne about *Gondal*, an island supposedly in the Pacific, but otherwise resembling the Haworth region.

Between 1835 and 1845 the girls made various attempts to go away and teach. Emily never settled away from home, and on three different occasions had to return to Haworth because her health broke down when she tried to live elsewhere. By 1844 all the sisters were at home, looking after their father, and trying to look after their brother when, in 1845, he was dismissed from his job and came to live at home, a pathetic drunkard and drug-addict. In spite of all this, or perhaps forced by the necessity for escape, the sisters began to write in earnest, and to publish. First, in 1846, a book of poems; this was printed at their own expense, and was a commercial failure. Then in October 1847, Charlotte published *Jane Eyre*, an immediate success: and in December *Wuthering Heights* and *Agnes Grey* followed.

Watching Branwell's deterioration, Anne pressed on with her second novel, *The Tenant of Wildfell Hall*, which was sent to the publishers in June 1848. In October Branwell died at last, and Emily immediately became ill, and died on December 19th. Anne, too, succumbed to T.B. and, having finished *Wildfell Hall*, died on May 28th, 1849. Charlotte and her father were left alone; Charlotte went on writing, and in October 1849 produced *Shirley*, in which she depicted Emily in the character of Shirley. *Villette* followed in 1853. In 1854 she married, but died in pregnancy in 1855. Her first novel, *The Professor*, which she had been revising, was published in 1857, and in the same year Mrs. Gaskell published her *Life of Charlotte Brontë*, still the classical biography, though many family details have been filled in and improved since. Last of all the family, Patrick Brontë died in 1861, at the age of 84.

The novels of Anne and Emily

Between them the two youngest Brontë sisters wrote three novels. Anne's two require little explanation. *Agnes Grey*, in first-person narrative, tells the story of a girl who takes employment as a governess, of her trials in her two posts, and of her courtship. The plot is very simple; the interest is sustained by Anne's narrative ability, shown in her descriptions of the sort of life a governess had to live, and the difficult people—both children and adults—she had to deal with, having little or no training, authority or equipment. Much of the story (though not the outcome) is autobiographical, at least in origin. *The Tenant of Wildfell Hall* is very different. Anne, having watched her

3

brother's pathetic decline from promise to drunkenness and death, felt she had a duty to show to the world the reality of such a life. The result was a novel which was much condemned on its first appearance for its author's supposed relish in describing unpalatable facts and unpleasant scenes. In form, it breaks into three parts. First the narrator, Gilbert Markham, meets a lady who has mysteriously taken up residence in a moorland house on the edge of his own land. He falls in love with her and she, unable to explain why she cannot accept him, gives him the manuscript of her diary which forms the second part of the novel. This shows her to be the wife of a gentleman from whom she had run away in desperation at his drunkenness and his mistresses. The third part, narrated by Markham again, brings her return to her husband when he falls ill, his death, and at last her marriage to Markham. The novel lacks the natural unity of *Agnes Grey*, and would have benefited from concentration. But it is driven along by the force of Anne's purpose, and most of all by her ability for subtle characterisation.

Wuthering Heights, Emily's only novel, is unlike any of the novels of her sisters, and unique in its kind. Of all the novels of passion which the nineteenth century produced in abundance, it is one of the few that maintain a hold on the modern reader. It belongs to its period and could probably not have been written at any other time, yet Emily was not to be caught out by the dangers of artificiality and false sentiment, always inherent in any set of conventions, and she writes a first novel with a strange imaginative power matched by a remarkable technique.

The action takes place in the southern Dales country

where Emily lived, but she does not tell the story of her life, or even of part of it. The characters, the plot and the shape of the whole book come from her imagination. There are two country houses—really large farmsteads —and two families, the Earnshaws at Wuthering Heights, and, at Thrushcross Grange, the Lintons—a little more educated and 'polite'. (For a family tree, showing the carefully planned relationships between the characters, see p. 13.) It is perhaps significant that, while *Linton* could be a family name anywhere in England, *Earnshaw* is a characteristically Northern name. The houses and their families are rooted in the history of the place but the stable pattern of their lives is disturbed by a strange little foundling boy, Heathcliff, a child of no home. As he grows up at the Heights he makes an enemy of the son of the house, Hindley, and an inseparable friend of the daughter, Cathy. (There are two Catherines, mother and daughter. The elder, beloved of Heathcliff, is in the editorial text of this volume referred to as *Cathy*, his familiar name for her. The daughter is *Catherine*. Emily Brontë uses the two names for the two characters interchangeably; since Cathy dies giving birth to Catherine there is no confusion in the novel.) As they approach adulthood, Heathcliff is maltreated by Hindley and finally feels himself rejected by Cathy, who becomes engaged to Edgar Linton, heir of the Grange. Heathcliff disappears, but returns years later, a self-made and brutally confident man, armed with a determination to gain control of both houses and revenge himself for all the ills he feels they have done him. His first steps are to run Hindley deep into gambling debts and to induce Edgar's sister, Isabella, to go through a runaway marriage with himself. Then he torments both

Hindley and Isabella. But he is driven also by an indestructible passion for Cathy, whose hold on him does not diminish even after her death in childbirth. He pursues his plan, using as tools all the inhabitants of the two houses, including Hindley's son, Hareton, and Cathy's daughter, another Catherine—but not his beloved Cathy herself, whom he cannot control during her life, or ignore when she is dead. He brings his plan of revenge to fulfilment, yet when it is virtually complete his mind is still captive to Cathy, who is in the true sense his 'femme fatale'. Everything else dwindles before her memory, which possesses him until he dies. The stranger who disrupted the two houses has gone, and the children, Hareton and young Catherine, are left to carry on the story of the Heights and the Grange.

The story is violent and often mysterious, but it is reduced to a degree of plausibility and almost normality by its narrator. She is Nelly Dean, maid and housekeeper at various times at either the Heights or the Grange, a down-to-earth Yorkshirewoman who takes everything in her stride. A major problem faced by any novelist is to decide how to narrate history. He will have much material and many incidents to retail, and it is extremely improbable that any one person would be able to be present at all of them. In a sense, he has to gather all the material of the story in one place, so that it can be convincingly assembled. In *Wuthering Heights*, two figures combine for this task. The story is opened by Lockwood, a gentleman on a visit from 'the South'. He is the gatherer of material, and the voice through whom the story is delivered, but he arrives on the scene only at the end of the long history. The author arranges that he shall hear the rest of it from Nelly, who has contrived over the years to be present at most of the important events, and has heard about the others direct from those who were there. Moreover, she belongs to that class invaluable to novelists, the servants, who can always be found concerned and watching, but need not be closely involved. Thus Lockwood learns almost the whole story from Nelly and presents it to the reader 'in her own words, only a little condensed' (ch. 15).

Emily and Anne Brontë and the Victorian novel

In some respects, Anne Brontë's two novels are typically Victorian. (Queen Victoria had been only ten years on the throne at the time of writing, and had scarcely impressed her character on it; although the age is named after her it had already developed its chief characteristics.) *Agnes Grey* deals with a well-mannered, retiring and modest young lady, who feels overcome with excitement when her lover even smiles at her. *Wildfell Hall* deals with a woman of much stronger character, who likes to theologise, who withers a would-be illicit lover with scorn, and will not even be seen with the hero in the most casual circumstances lest her character be blighted. Yet *Wildfell Hall* earned much moral disapproval in 1849, for its supposed morbidity in treating the decline of a drunkard so directly.

Wuthering Heights is more full of drama than either of Anne's novels. On the surface, it is as strictly 'moral' as any genteel Victorian could desire; but the surface is thin. Heathcliff openly shows his passion for Cathy after her marriage to Edgar Linton, and returns to hang about her house without any pretence. Cathy, on her part, as openly displays his attraction for her; she does not desert or neglect Edgar for Heathcliff, or intend to do so, but she clearly shows that she considers her marriage a convenience—a pleasant enough one—but not a matter to take her away from Heathcliff. Yet, except for Nelly's strictures in ch. 9—and these are well separated from the climax of the affair in ch. 11—Emily does not show much strictly moral disapproval of this behaviour. That it is disastrous, auguring long anguish for all concerned, is made very clear; that it is wrong, immoral, is not stressed. Cathy's selfishness and spite are presented with disapproval; her love affairs are merely fate. Yet notice that, for all the passion between her and Heathcliff, Emily never repels her own audience by overstepping the mark of Victorian propriety. It is, indeed, a considerable achievement to make the passion appear so fierce with so little material, as it were, though passion is, after all, psychological rather than physical.

The twentieth century prides itself on its ability to consider love and passion in the cold light of fact and reason, but is much more afraid of death than the Victorians were. The 'death-bed scene' is notoriously a favourite feature of Victorian novels—an opportunity for tearful forgiveness, sentiment and more or less trite moralising. It is interesting to see how Emily and Anne handle this tradition. In *Wildfell Hall* Arthur Huntingdon kills himself with drink; the invalid is not the conventional apathetic wraith of his former self but a cantankerous and demanding patient, whose behaviour makes us sympathise—perhaps for the first time without reservations—with the wife who has to nurse him. He dies, not romantically with a smile on his lips, but in terror; and his body is so corrupted that 'the coffin must be closed as soon as possible'.

Wuthering Heights has many deaths. A few are merely due to the passage of time—the first Mr. Earnshaw dies quietly one evening in his arm-chair. But of the main characters, the deaths of Hindley and Isabella 'off-stage', and of Cathy, Edgar, Linton Heathcliff and Heathcliff himself are all of importance in the development. This is no mere morbidity. Disease was a dangerous enemy; the consumption which was visibly wasting Linton carried off the Brontë sisters themselves, one after another. Today early death seems a wrong in nature; then it was a common fact of life, and the death-bed scene owes its existence to this. Of the four deaths which closely concern the reader, only Heathcliff's is extraordinary; and only one, Edgar's, bears any resemblance to the traditional 'death-bed scene'—in extremely abbreviated form. Linton's death in ch. 30 is a midnight horror for young Catherine; the elder Catherine dies, not in sentimental resignation, but after a scene of passionate recrimination with her lover (ch. 15). Heathcliff, by contrast, dies silently and alone, in the bed where Lockwood had dreamed of Catherine. Thus at almost every point the normal Victorian expectations are frustrated.

Except in one way. The story ends with Hareton and Catherine hand in hand. Emily Brontë has a major problem here; to avoid, after the passion of the bulk of the novel, an ultimate relapse into sentimentality. She has two means of avoiding this. The first is to present an example of foolish romantic attachment, and show the distance between it and real love. Lockwood arrives at

Wuthering Heights in ch. 1 as a self-described misanthrope, and it is part of his characterisation that the reader is made to realise the actual shallowness of his emotions. He then goes on to believe himself to be enamoured of Catherine; and so the reader sees the difference between this superficial man's imagined affections, and the real if incoherent feelings of Hareton. Besides, there is a proportion in the development of all art which must be observed; in the case of this novel it requires that Heathcliff's plan, so long in designing and execution, should be frustrated at last, and this can only be by the union of the couple he had so confidently determined to alienate from one another.

Scheme of extracts

The extracts have been chosen, not in order to present a settled interpretation of the 'meaning' of the novels, but to show the different aspects of the novelist's art, and to lead the reader into an understanding of the writers and their books. *Wuthering Heights*, much the most considerable novel of the three, naturally receives the fullest treatment. It is a novel which can be interpreted in many ways, and each reader will be affected differently. The extracts that follow are designed to introduce the reader, first to the background of the novel, and then to the various techniques used by Emily Brontë to develop her plot. This order is chosen rather than the reverse, because such features as characterisation, narrative method and realism in dialogue must always be understood in relation to a particular novel. There is no one way in which a novelist is to handle these, and no single set of criteria for judging them. Anne's novels are simpler than *Wuthering Heights*, and a simpler scheme of extracts suffices to introduce them. The reader who must follow one or the other author alone may isolate the respective groups of extracts, but the comparison provided here will be found more satisfactory in bringing out the distinctive qualities of the two sisters.

On the text of 'Wuthering Heights'

The first edition of 1847 was received with dismay by the two sisters (*Agnes Grey* formed a third volume) on account of the many faults in its printing. This was made the excuse for considerable revision of punctuation, paragraphing, etc., in the 1850 edition which Charlotte supervised, and this has become the standard text. But the faults of the 1847 edition are obvious, and are largely due to careless proof-reading; Charlotte had no need to 'improve' the text as she has done. This edition, therefore, uses the text of the first edition of 1847, with its characteristic vitality of punctuation, only correcting the self-evident errors, which are few.

The families of 'Wuthering Heights'

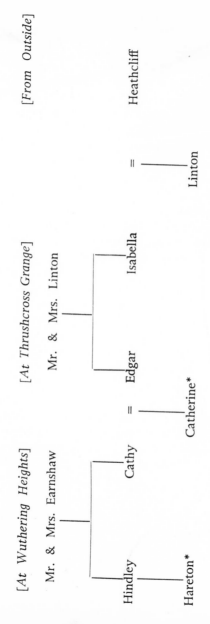

[At Wuthering Heights]   [At Thrushcross Grange]   [From Outside]

Mr. & Mrs. Earnshaw   Mr. & Mrs. Linton

Hindley   Cathy   Edgar   Isabella   Heathcliff

                    =   =

Catherine*   Linton

Hareton*

* The two survivors at the close of the novel. Their forthcoming marriage, uniting the two families, is clearly envisaged (Linton Heathcliff, Catherine's boy-husband, having died).

'Wuthering Heights': the background of normal life

Wuthering Heights is a story of the interaction of the inhabitants of two houses in two generations, and of the impact on them of the outsider Heathcliff. In order to understand the force of this impact, we need to know what normality is like. The first extract shows one of the houses, Wuthering Heights itself, in a normal state of contented domesticity. In the first chapter of the book, Emily Brontë describes the normal farmhouse, but only as a preface to a scene which is far from normal. To find this 'normality' we have to turn to the end of the book, where (in ch. 32, from which extract 1 is taken) the house has returned to its apparently natural happiness after Heathcliff's death.

The extract illustrates another kind of 'normality' also—the kind of 'love-interest' expected by Victorian readers. To us, this may seen too commonplace, even sentimental; in its place in the novel, however, it appears differently. One of the most important features of any kind of extended composition, whether novel, poem or play, is that the aspect of any incident changes according to its position in the scheme or plot. What has led up to it, where it is, what is about to happen, all increase and affect its meaning and influence on the reader. Alone, this scene between Catherine and Hareton may seem tame or trite, though the author takes precautions against this; but after the stormy history of Heathcliff it comes as a welcome return to normality.

In this extract, the speaker is Lockwood, who is tenant of Thrushcross Grange, though he has not lived there for months (see Introduction, p. 6). He does not know, therefore, that Heathcliff, his landlord, who lived at Wuthering Heights, is dead, until Nelly Dean tells him. During his previous stay she had been housekeeper at the Grange; hence his surprise to find her at the Heights. (For her importance in the novel, see Introduction, p. 6.)

I

A sudden impulse seized me to visit Thrushcross Grange. It was scarcely noon, and I conceived that I might as well pass the night under my own roof, as in an inn. Besides, I could spare a day easily, to arrange matters with my landlord, and thus save myself the trouble of invading the neighbourhood again.

Having rested a while, I directed my servant to inquire the way to the village; and, with great fatigue to our beasts, we managed the distance in some three hours.

I left him there, and proceeded down the valley alone. The grey church looked greyer, and the lonely churchyard lonelier. I distinguished a moor sheep cropping the short turf on the graves. It was sweet, warm weather—too warm for travelling; but the heat did not hinder me from enjoying the delightful scenery above and below; had I seen it nearer August[1], I'm sure it would have tempted me to waste a month among its solitudes. In winter, nothing more dreary, in summer, nothing more divine, than those glens shut in by hills, and those bluff, bold swells of heath.

I reached the Grange before sunset, and knocked for admittance; but the family had retreated into the back premises, I judged by one thin, blue wreath curling from the kitchen chimney, and they did not hear.

I rode into the court. Under the porch, a girl of nine or ten sat knitting, and an old woman reclined on the house-steps, smoking a meditative pipe.

'Is Mrs. Dean within?' I demanded of the dame.

'Mistress Dean? Nay!' she answered, 'shoo doesn't bide here: shoo's up at th' Heights.'

'Are you the housekeeper, then?' I continued.

'Eea, Aw keep th' hause,' she replied.

'Well, I'm Mr. Lockwood, the master—Are there any rooms to lodge me in, I wonder? I wish to stay here all night.'

'T' maister!' she cried in astonishment. 'Whet, whoiver knew yah wur coming? Yah sud ha' send word! They's nowt norther dry—nor mensful abaht t' place—nowt there isn't!'

She threw down her pipe and bustled in, the girl followed, and I entered too; soon perceiving that her report was true, and, moreover, that I had almost upset her wits by my unwelcome apparition.

I bid her be composed—I would go out for a walk; and, meantime, she must try to prepare a corner of a sitting-room for me to sup in, and a bed-room to sleep in. No sweeping and dusting, only good fires and dry sheets were necessary.

She seemed willing to do her best; though she thrust the hearth-brush into the grates in mistake for the poker; and malappropriated several other articles of her craft;

but I retired, confiding in her energy for a resting-place against my return.

Wuthering Heights was the goal of my proposed excursion. An after-thought brought me back, when I had quitted the court.

'All well at the Heights?' I inquired of the woman.

'Eea, f'r owt Ee knaw!' she answered, skurrying away with a pan of hot cinders.

I would have asked why Mrs. Dean had deserted the Grange; but it was impossible to delay her at such a crisis, so I turned away and made my exit, rambling leisurely along, with the glow of a sinking sun behind, and the mild glory of a rising moon in front; one fading, and the other brightening, as I quitted the park, and climbed the stony by-road off to Mr. Heathcliff's dwelling.

Before I arrived in sight of it, all that remained of day was a beamless amber light along the west; but I could see every pebble on the path, and every blade of grass, by that splendid moon.

I had neither to climb the gate, nor to knock—it yielded to my hand.

That is an improvement! I thought. And I noticed another, by the aid of my nostrils; a fragrance of stocks and wall flowers, wafted on the air, from amongst the homely fruit trees.

Both doors and lattices were open; and, yet, as is usually the case in a coal district[2], a fine, red fire illumined the chimney; the comfort which the eye derives from it, renders the extra heat endurable. But the house of Wuthering Heights is so large, that the inmates have plenty of space for withdrawing out of its influence; and, accordingly, what inmates there were had stationed themselves not far from one of the windows. I could both see them and hear them talk before I entered; and looked and listened in consequence, being moved thereto by a mingled sense of curiosity, and envy that grew as I lingered.

'Con-*trary*!' said a voice, as sweet as a silver bell—'That for the third time, you dunce! I'm not going to tell you, again—Recollect, or I pull your hair!'

'Contrary, then,' answered another, in deep, but softened tones. 'And now, kiss me, for minding so well.'

'No, read it over first correctly, without a single mistake.'

The male speaker began to read—he was a young man, respectably dressed, and seated at a table, having a book before him. His handsome features glowed with pleasure, and his eyes kept impatiently wandering from the page to a small white hand over his shoulder, which recalled him by a smart slap on the cheek, whenever its owner detected such signs of inattention.

Its owner stood behind; her light shining ringlets blending, at intervals, with his own brown locks, as she bent to superintend his studies; and her face—it was lucky he could not see her face, or he would never have been so steady—I could, and I bit my lip, in spite, at having thrown away the chance I might have had[3], of doing something besides staring at its smiting beauty.

The task was done, not free from further blunders, but the pupil claimed a reward and received at least five kisses, which, however, he generously returned. Then, they came to the door, and from their conversation, I judged they were about to issue out and have a walk on the moors. I supposed I should be condemned in Hareton Earnshaw's heart, if not by his mouth, to the lowest pit in the infernal regions if I showed my unfortunate person in his neighbourhood then; and feeling very mean and malignant, I skulked round to seek refuge in the kitchen.

There was unobstructed admittance on that side also;

and, at the door, sat my old friend, Nelly Dean, sewing and singing a song, which was often interrupted from within, by harsh words[4] of scorn and intolerance, uttered in far from musical accents.

'Aw'd rayther, by th' haulf, hev 'em swearing i' my lugs frough morn tuh neeght, nur hearken yah, hahsiver!' said the tenant of the kitchen, in answer to an unheard speech of Nelly's. 'It's a blazing shaime, ut Aw cannut oppen t' Blessed Book, bud yah set up them glories tuh sattan, un' all t' flaysome wickedness ut iver wer born intuh t'warld! Oh! yah're a raight nowt; un' shoo's another; un' that poor lad 'ull be lost, atween ye. Poor lad!' he added, with a groan; 'he's witched, Aw'm sartin on 't! O, Lord, judge 'em, fur they's norther law nur justice amang wer rullers!'

'No! or we should be sitting in flaming fagots, I suppose,' retorted the singer. 'But wisht, old man, and read your Bible, like a christian, and never mind me. This is "Fairy Annie's Wedding"—a bonny tune—it goes to a dance.'

Mrs. Dean was about to recommence, when I advanced, and recognising me directly, she jumped to her feet, crying—

'Why, bless you, Mr. Lockwood! How could you think of returning in this way? All's shut up at Thrushcross Grange. You should have given us notice!'

'I've arranged to be accommodated there, for as long as I shall stay,' I answered. 'I depart again to-morrow.'

Wuthering Heights, ch. 32

Notes

[1] *nearer August*: This scene takes place in September; Lockwood's only other visit was at the back end of the year.

[2] *a coal district*: This was a farming district, but coal was mined in the region.

[3] *the chance I might have had*: Lockwood never had a chance (see extract 2), but entertained a romantic, but noticeably ineffectual, notion that he might court Catherine and carry her off.

[4] *harsh words*: spoken by Joseph, the bigoted old servant.

lugs: ears.

sattan: Satan.

flaysome: terrible.

Emily Brontë may give the impression of writing 'straight from the heart'. Yet a careful study of the passage soon shows that she knew what she was about. No good writer despises technique—the calculation of desired results and the methods necessary to produce them, the effect of visual changes, changes of pace, and the like. Many details add together to make a total effect.

A study of this passage might begin by considering the oblique approach made to this scene. Emily Brontë wants to show the happiness of the new atmosphere at Wuthering Heights. But she starts, not there, but with Lockwood miles away, travelling to Scotland, and turning off his route almost by accident. Then the approach which follows is still gradual, and its steps should be followed, for each of them contains some new point. The scene is enlarged and developed by other means than the travel of the mind's eye: for example, by the characteristic behaviour of various people; by gentleness of movement (but not monotony); and by the ineffective grotesqueness of Joseph (who is unseen). Attempt to find some detail which is not used in some way, and you will see that there are very few.

The headnote says that the apparent sentimentality of the central scene of the two lovers is dispelled when the passage falls into its context. One might question whether it is altogether avoided; or again, if it matters. But in any case, the author has built into Lockwood's presentation a kind of folly which is plainly intended to set off the genuineness of the feeling between Hareton and Catherine.

The background of nature

Normal human life was disrupted in the two houses by Heathcliff; but the moors between and beyond remained undisturbed. As Lockwood said (see extract 1): 'in winter, nothing more dreary, in summer, nothing more divine'— but always a silent, unchanging contrast to the turbulence of the short-lived humans who move across them. Moor-land countryside is commonly thought of as bleak; it is the more important to realise, then, that to Emily Brontë (in spite of the snowstorm in chs. 2-3), it was essentially a region of freedom and delight, of escape from the confinement of close houses. The moors bring a sense of beauty, not of depression. For bleak moors we must turn to Anne's *Wildfell Hall* (extract 5, p. 36): two brief but important extracts will show Emily's view.

Nelly Dean is speaking of Catherine, the younger, who is not allowed to go near Wuthering Heights because it belongs to Heathcliff, the enemy of her father, Edgar Linton. Gimmerton is the village nearest the Grange, where the Lintons lived.

2

Till she reached the age of thirteen, she had not once been

beyond the range of the park by herself. Mr. Linton would take her with him, a mile or so outside, on rare occasions; but he trusted her to no one else. Gimmerton was an unsubstantial name in her ears; the chapel, the only building she had approached or entered, except her own home. Wuthering Heights and Mr. Heathcliff did not exist for her; she was a perfect recluse; and, apparently perfectly contented. Sometimes, indeed, while surveying the country from her nursery window, she would observe—

'Ellen, how long will it be before I can walk to the top of those hills? I wonder what lies on the other side—is it the sea?'

'No, Miss Cathy,' I would answer, 'it is hills again just like these.'

'And what are those golden rocks like, when you stand under them?' she once asked.

The abrupt descent of Penistone Craggs particularly attracted her notice, especially when the setting sun shone on it, and the topmost heights; and the whole extent of landscape besides lay in shadow.

I explained that they were bare masses of stone, with hardly enough earth in their clefts to nourish a stunted tree.

'And why are they bright so long after it is evening here?' she pursued.

'Because they are a great deal higher up than we are,' replied I; 'you could not climb them, they are too high and steep. In winter the frost is always there before it comes to us; and, deep into summer, I have found snow under that black hollow on the north-east side!'

'Oh, you have been on them!' she cried, gleefully. 'Then I can go, too, when I am a woman. Has papa been, Ellen?'

'Papa would tell you, Miss,' I answered, hastily, 'that they are not worth the trouble of visiting. The moors,

23

where you ramble with him, are much nicer; and Thrush-cross park is the finest place in the world.'

'But I know the park, and I don't know those,' she murmured to herself. 'And I should delight to look round me, from the brow of that tallest point—my little pony, Minny, shall take me sometime.'

One of the maids mentioning the Fairy Cave, quite turned her head with a desire to fulfil this project; she teased Mr. Linton about it; and he promised she should have the journey when she got older: but Miss Catherine measured her age by months, and—

'Now, am I old enough to go to Penistone Craggs?' was the constant question in her mouth.

The road thither wound close by Wuthering Heights. Edgar had not the heart to pass it; so she received as constantly the answer.

'Not yet, love, not yet.'

Wuthering Heights, ch. 18

*

The speaker below is the young Catherine, again. Linton is Heathcliff's son, Catherine's cousin (Heathcliff had eloped with Edgar Linton's sister Isabella). Heathcliff has induced Catherine to visit the Heights, as part of his plan to marry her to Linton and obtain her inheritance.

3

'Linton sat in the arm-chair, and I in the little rocking chair on the hearth-stone, and we laughed and talked so merrily, and found so much to say; we planned where we would go, and what we would do in summer. I needn't repeat that, because you would call it silly.

'One time, however, we were near quarrelling. He said

24

the pleasantest manner of spending a hot July day was lying from morning till evening on a bank of heath in the middle of the moors, with the bees humming dreamily about among the bloom, and the larks singing high up over head, and the blue sky and bright sun shining steadily and cloudlessly. That was his most perfect idea of heaven's happiness—mine was rocking in a rustling green tree, with a west wind blowing, and bright, white clouds flitting rapidly above; and not only larks, but throstles, and blackbirds, and linnets, and cuckoos pouring out music on every side, and the moors seen at a distance, broken into cool dusky dells; but close by great swells of long grass undulating in waves to the breeze; and woods and sounding water, and the whole world awake and wild with joy. He wanted all to lie in an ecstasy of peace; I wanted all to sparkle, and dance in a glorious jubilee.'

Wuthering Heights, ch. 24

That Emily Brontë loved her moors is very plain from these passages; the variety of mood they display may be found here, in at least four different ways. But she does not write of them only for this reason. Scenery has no meaning of its own; it takes an emotional colouring according to the mood and character of the onlooker. Here it is used dramatically, as well as (in the second extract) to show character. The crags in the first extract are distant, unknown, rocky and bare; the way to them winds past Wuthering Heights; the home park is quiet, beautiful and peaceful. In this way Emily Brontë gives real meaning to mere beauty.

The inhabitants of 'Wuthering Heights'

The extracts so far have shown a world of friendly, hard-working farms-people living in a tough but attractive environment. That is Emily Brontë's idea of normal Dales life; but the picture she presents at the beginning of the novel is very different from this. The southern gentleman, Lockwood, who comes north with a romantic desire to 'get away from it all' after the failure of a mild love-affair (which he takes more seriously than a sensible man ought) finds himself in the midst of an incomprehensible set of people, sour and unhelpful, who speak to him to suggest that they would as soon see him go as come. The following scene illustrates this; and further, it illustrates the characters of several of the most important figures in the book. The younger Catherine, beautiful but tart, afraid of Heathcliff but scornful of everyone: Hareton, unservile but living like a labourer: Heathcliff himself, careless of everyone, the master feared by all: and Joseph, the grotesque old man, summing up in himself and his dialect the roughness and unfriendliness of the place. Yet these are the people whom Lockwood finds, a short year later, but at the end of the story, in the happy situation of the first extract—all but Heathcliff. In his absence lies the story.

Lockwood, the narrator, himself is well displayed in this extract. He is the urbane gentleman, at ease in company, gallant to ladies, confident with men : yet now he is thrown off balance at every turn, and his gallantry becomes comedy and mere silliness. His sophistication may be very well 'in town', but it cannot cope with such downrightness, least of all with the roughness of Wuthering Heights. (Emily Brontë, as Charlotte's portrait of her as Shirley in *Shirley* suggests, was full of local patriotism. The only other product of 'the south, somewhere near London', in *Wuthering Heights* is Linton Heathcliff, a selfish, spoilt mother's darling. Heathcliff himself is not one of those, but he is not a local product either : in the last chapter Nelly Dean wonders, 'Where did he come from, the little dark thing, harboured by a good man to this bane?')

4

I took my hat, and, after a four miles' walk, arrived at Heathcliff's garden gate just in time to escape the first feathery flakes of a snow shower.

On that bleak hill-top the earth was hard with a black frost, and the air made me shiver through every limb. Being unable to remove the chain, I jumped over, and, running up the flagged causeway bordered with straggling gooseberry bushes, knocked vainly for admittance, till my knuckles tingled, and the dogs howled.

'Wretched inmates!' I ejaculated, mentally, 'you deserve perpetual isolation from your species for your churlish inhospitality. At least, I would not keep my doors barred in the day time—I don't care—I will get in!'

So resolved, I grasped the latch, and shook it vehemently.

Vinegear-faced Joseph projected his head from a round window of the barn.

'Whet are ye for?' he shouted. 'T' maister's dahn i' t' fowld. Goa rahned by th' end ut' laith[1], if yah went tuh spake tull him.'

'Is there nobody inside to open the door?' I hallooed, responsively.

'They's nobbut t' missis; and shoo'll nut oppen 't and ye mak yer flaysome dins till neeght.'

'Why? cannot you tell her who I am, eh, Joseph?'

'Nor-ne me! Aw'll hae noa hend wi't,' muttered the head, vanishing.

The snow began to drive thickly. I seized the handle to essay another trial; when a young man, without coat, and shouldering a pitchfork, appeared in the yard behind. He hailed me to follow him, and, after marching through a washhouse, and a paved area containing a coal-shed, pump, and pigeon cote, we at length arrived in the large, warm, cheerful apartment, where I was formerly received.

It glowed delightfully in the radiance of an immense fire, compounded of coal, peat, and wood: and near the table, laid for a plentiful evening meal, I was pleased to observe the 'missis', an individual whose existence I had never previously suspected.

I bowed and waited, thinking she would bid me take a seat. She looked at me, leaning back in her chair, and remained motionless and mute.

'Rough weather!' I remarked. 'I'm afraid, Mrs. Heathcliff, the door must bear the consequence of your servants' leisure attendance: I had hard work to make them hear me!'

She never opened her mouth. I stared—she stared also. At any rate, she kept her eyes on me, in a cool, regardless manner, exceedingly embarrassing and disagreeable.

'Sit down,' said the young man, gruffly. 'He'll be in soon.'

I obeyed; and hemmed, and called the villain Juno[2], who deigned, at this second interview, to move the extreme tip of her tail, in token of owning my acquaintance.

'A beautiful animal!' I commenced again. 'Do you intend parting with the little ones, madam?'

'They are not mine,' said the amiable hostess more repellingly than Heathcliff himself could have replied.

'Ah, your favourites are among these!' I continued, turning to an obscure cushion full of something like cats.

'A strange choice of favourites,' she observed scornfully.

Unluckily, it was a heap of dead rabbits—I hemmed once more, and drew closer to the hearth, repeating my comment on the wildness of the evening.

'You should not have come out,' she said, rising and reaching from the chimney-piece two of the painted canisters.

Her position before was sheltered from the light: now, I had a distinct view of her whole figure and countenance. She was slender, and apparently scarcely past girlhood: an admirable form, and the most exquisite little face that I have ever had the pleasure of beholding: small features, very fair; flaxen ringlets, or rather golden, hanging loose on her delicate neck; and eyes—had they been agreeable in expression, they would have been irresistible—fortunately for my susceptible heart, the only sentiment they evinced hovered between scorn and a kind of desperation, singularly unnatural to be detected there.

The canisters were almost out of her reach; I made a motion to aid her; she turned upon me as a miser might turn, if any one attempted to assist him in counting his gold.

'I don't want your help,' she snapped, 'I can get them for myself.'

'I beg your pardon,' I hastened to reply.

'Were you asked to tea?' she demanded, tying an apron over her neat black frock, and standing with a spoonful of the leaf poised over the pot.

'I shall be glad to have a cup,' I answered.

'Were you asked?' she repeated.

'No,' I said, half smiling. 'You are the proper person to ask me.'

She flung the tea back, spoon and all, and resumed her chair in a pet, her forehead corrugated, and her red under-lip pushed out, like a child's, ready to cry.

Meanwhile, the young man had slung onto his person a decidedly shabby upper garment, and, erecting himself before the blaze, looked down on me, from the corner of his eyes, for all the world as if there were some mortal feud unavenged between us. I began to doubt whether he were a servant or not; his dress and speech were both rude, entirely devoid of the superiority observable in Mr. and Mrs. Heathcliff; his thick, brown curls were rough and uncultivated, his whiskers encroached bearishly over his cheeks, and his hands were embrowned like those of a common labourer: still his bearing was free, almost haughty; and he showed none of a domestic's assiduity in attending on the lady of the house.

In the absence of clear proofs of his condition, I deemed it best to abstain from noticing his curious conduct, and, five minutes afterwards, the entrance of Heathcliff relieved me, in some measure, from my uncomfortable state.

'You see, sir, I am come according to promise!' I exclaimed, assuming the cheerful 'and I fear I shall be weather-bound for half an hour, if you can afford me shelter during that space'.

'Half an hour?' he said, shaking the white flakes from his clothes; 'I wonder you should select the thick of a snow-storm to ramble about in. Do you know that you run a risk of being lost in the marshes? People familiar with these moors often miss their road on such evenings, and, I can tell you, there is no chance of a change at present.'

'Perhaps I can get a guide among your lads, and he might stay at the Grange till morning—could you spare me one?'

'No, I could not.'

'Oh, indeed! Well, then, I must trust to my own sagacity.'

'Umph!'

'Are you going to mak' th' tea?' demanded he of the shabby coat, shifting his ferocious gaze from me to the young lady.

'Is *he* to have any?' she asked, appealing to Heathcliff.

'Get it ready, will you?' was the answer, uttered so savagely that I started. The tone in which the words were said, revealed a genuine bad nature. I no longer felt inclined to call Heathcliff a capital fellow.

When the preparations were finished, he invited me with—

'Now, sir, bring forward your chair.' And we all, including the rustic youth, drew round the table, an austere silence prevailing while we discussed our meal[3].

I thought, if I had caused the cloud, it was my duty to make an effort to dispel it. They could not every day sit so grim and taciturn, and it was impossible, however illtempered they might be, that the universal scowl they wore was their everyday countenance.

'It is strange,' I began in the interval of swallowing one cup of tea and receiving another, 'it is strange how custom can mould our tastes and ideas; many could not imagine the existence of happiness in a life of such complete exile from the world as you spend, Mr. Heathcliff; yet, I'll venture to say, that, surrounded by your family, and with your amiable lady as the presiding genius over your home and heart—'

'My amiable lady!' he interrupted, with an almost diabolical sneer on his face. 'Where is she—my amiable lady?'

'Mrs. Heathcliff, your wife, I mean.'

'Well, yes—Oh! you would intimate that her spirit has taken the post of ministering angel, and guards the fortunes of Wuthering Heights, even when her body is gone. Is that it?'

Perceiving myself in a blunder, I attempted to correct it. I might have seen that there was too great a disparity between the ages of the parties to make it likely that they were man and wife. One was about forty; a period of mental vigour at which men seldom cherish the delusion of being married for love, by girls: that dream is reserved for the solace of our declining years. The other did not look seventeen.

Then it flashed upon me—'The clown at my elbow, who is drinking his tea out of a basin, and eating his bread with unwashed hands, may be her husband. Heathcliff, junior, of course. Here is the consequence of being buried alive: she has thrown herself away upon that boor, from sheer ignorance that better individuals existed! A sad pity—I must beware how I cause her to regret her choice.'

The last reflection may seem conceited; it was not. My neighbour struck me as bordering on repulsive. I knew, through experience, that I was tolerably attractive.

'Mrs. Heathcliff is my daughter-in-law,' said Heathcliff, corroborating my surmise. He turned, as he spoke, a peculiar look in her direction, a look of hatred unless he has a most perverse set of facial muscles that will not, like those of other people, interpret the language of his soul.

'Ah, certainly—I see now; you are the favoured possessor

of the beneficent fairy,' I remarked, turning to my neighbour.

This was worse than before: the youth grew crimson, and clenched his fist with every appearance of a meditated assault. But he seemed to recollect himself, presently; and smothered the storm in a brutal curse, muttered on my behalf, which, however, I took care not to notice.

'Unhappy in your conjectures, sir!' observed my host; 'we neither of us have the privilege of owning your good fairy; her mate is dead. I said she was my daughter-in-law, therefore, she must have married my son.'

'And this young man is—'

'Not my son, assuredly!'

Heathcliff smiled again, as if it were rather too bold a jest to attribute the paternity of that bear to him.

'My name is Hareton Earnshaw,' growled the other; 'and I'd counsel you to respect it!'

'I've shown no disrespect,' was my reply, laughing internally at the dignity with which he announced himself.

He fixed his eye on me no longer than I cared to return the stare, for fear I might be tempted either to box his ears, or render my hilarity audible. I began to feel unmistakably out of place in that pleasant family circle. The dismal spiritual atmosphere overcame, and more than neutralised the glowing physical comforts round me; and I resolved to be cautious how I ventured under those rafters a third time.

The business of eating being concluded, and no one uttering a word of sociable conversation, I approached a window to examine the weather.

A sorrowful sight I saw; dark night coming down prematurely, and sky and hills mingled in one bitter whirl of wind and suffocating snow.

'I don't think it possible for me to get home now, without a guide,' I could not help exclaiming. 'The roads will be buried already; and if they were bare, I could scarcely distinguish a foot in advance.'

'Hareton, drive those dozen sheep into the barn porch. They'll be covered if left in the fold all night; and put a plank before them,' said Heathcliff.

'How must I do?' I continued, with rising irritation.

There was no reply to my question; and on looking round, I saw only Joseph bringing in a pail of porridge for the dogs; and Mrs. Heathcliff, leaning over the fire, diverting herself with burning a bundle of matches which had fallen from the chimney-piece as she restored the tea-canister to its place.

Wuthering Heights, ch. 2

Notes
  [1] *laith*: barn.
  [2] *Juno*: a fierce bitch, which had attacked Lockwood during his first visit.
  [3] *discussed our meal*: 'investigated' it—a common, almost flippant nineteenth-century expression.

This is a very interesting scene, for the light it throws on the author's technique in several ways. A comparison of this and the first extract is very rewarding, both in what it can show about her methods of developing the scene, and in building up the atmosphere of the place—this last being particularly important in the development of the book as a whole. The characters are balanced against one another in appearance, behaviour and reaction; their arrival is as significant as if this were a play, and the characters were to step on to a stage. Such details as the fire, the rabbits, the tea-caddy, Heathcliff's injunction, 'Hareton, drive those dozen sheep into the barn porch', are more than mere 'local colour'; they are dramatically significant. And beyond the passage itself, a reading of the whole novel will show how it contains the whole book in miniature—except for the final unravelling, which is saved for the last chapter.

Anne Brontë's style

The first extract from Anne Brontë's *The Tenant of Wild-fell Hall* illustrates two themes. The first is the moorland scenery in its wilder aspect—scarcely to be found in *Wuthering Heights*, as the previous extract shows. The second is Anne Brontë's skill in narration. The two run together, because it is important that the wild scenery is the setting for Markham's first meeting with a lady whom he might expect to find in more elegant surroundings, and whose presence in this obscure place has already made him curious. The ensuing action has a liveliness unusual in Anne Brontë, whose incidents generally take the form of encounters of personality rather than of physical action. Nevertheless, it is skilfully done, with its alternation of action and suspense, suddenness and quiet, the expected and the unexpected, friendliness and fear.

5

I was out with my dog and gun, in pursuit of such game as I could find within the territory of Linden-Car; but finding none at all, I turned my arms against the hawks and carrion-crows, whose depredations, as I suspected, had deprived me of better prey. To this end, I left the more frequented regions, the wooded valleys, the corn-fields and the meadow lands, and proceeded to mount the steep acclivity of Wildfell, the wildest and the loftiest eminence in our neighbourhood, where, as you ascend, the hedges, as well as the trees, become scanty and stunted, the former, at length, giving place to rough stone fences, partly greened over with ivy and moss, the latter to larches and Scotch fir-trees, or isolated blackthorns. The fields, being rough and stony, and wholly unfit for the plough, were mostly devoted to the pasturing of sheep and cattle; the soil was thin and poor: bits of grey rock here and there peeped out from the grassy hillocks; bilberry plants and heather—relics of more savage wildness—grew under the walls; and in many of the enclosures, ragweeds and rushes usurped supremacy over the scanty herbage;—but these were not my property.

Near the top of this hill, about two miles from Linden-Car, stood Wildfell Hall, a superannuated mansion of the Elizabethan era, built of dark grey stone—venerable and picturesque to look at, but, doubtless, cold and gloomy enough to inhabit, with its thick stone mullions and little latticed panes, its time-eaten air-holes, and its too lonely, too unsheltered situation—only shielded from the war of wind and weather by a group of Scotch firs, themselves half blighted with storms, and looking as stern and gloomy as the Hall itself. Behind it lay a few desolated fields, and then, the brown heath-clad summit of the hill; before it (enclosed by stone walls, and entered by an iron gate with large balls of grey granite—similar to those which decorated the roof and gables—surmounting the gate-posts) was a garden—once stocked with such hardy plants and flowers as could best brook the soil and climate, and such trees and shrubs as could best endure the gardener's torturing shears, and most readily assume the shapes he chose to give them—now, having been left so many years, untilled and untrimmed, abandoned to the weeds and the grass, to the frost and the wind, the rain and the drought, it presented a very singular appearance indeed. The close green walls of privet, that had bordered the principal walk, were two-thirds withered away, and the rest grown beyond all reasonable bounds; the old boxwood swan, that sat beside the scraper, had lost its neck and half its body; the castellated towers of laurel in the middle of the garden, the gigantic warrior that stood on one side of the gateway, and the lion that guarded the other, were sprouted into such fantastic shapes as resembled nothing either in heaven or earth, or in the waters under earth; but, to my young imagination, they presented all of them a goblinish appearance, that harmonised well with the ghostly legends and dark traditions our old nurse had told us respecting the haunted Hall and its departed occupants.

I had succeeded in killing a hawk and two crows when I came within sight of the mansion; and then, relinquishing further depredations, I sauntered on, to have a look at the old place, and see what changes had been wrought in it by its new inhabitant. I did not like to go quite to the front and stare in at the gate; but I paused beside the garden wall, and looked, and saw no change—except in one wing, where the broken windows and dilapidated roof had evidently been repaired, and where a thin wreath of smoke was curling up from the stack of chimneys.

While I thus stood, leaning on my gun, and looking up at the dark gables, sunk in an idle reverie, weaving a tissue of wayward fancies, in which old associations and the fair young hermit, now within those walls, bore a nearly equal part, I heard a slight rustling and scrambling just within the garden; and, glancing in the direction whence the sound proceeded, I beheld a tiny hand elevated above the wall; it clung to the topmost stone, and then another little hand was raised to take a firmer hold, and then appeared a small white forehead, surmounted with wreaths of light brown hair, with a pair of deep blue eyes beneath, and the upper portion of a diminutive ivory nose.

The eyes did not notice me, but sparkled with glee on beholding Sancho, my beautiful black and white setter, that was coursing about the field with its muzzle to the ground. The little creature raised its face and called aloud to the dog. The good-natured animal paused, looked up, and wagged his tail, but made no further advances. The child (a little boy, apparently about five years old) scrambled up to the top of the wall, and called again and again; but finding this of no avail, apparently made up his mind, like Mahomet, to go to the mountain, since the mountain would not come to him, and attempted to get over; but a crabbed old cherry tree, that grew hard by, caught him by the frock, in one of its crooked scraggy arms that stretched over the wall. In attempting to disengage himself, his foot slipped, and down he tumbled—but not to the earth;— the tree still kept him suspended. There was a silent struggle, and then a piercing shriek; but, in an instant, I had dropped my gun on the grass, and caught the little fellow in my arms.

I wiped his eyes with his frock, told him he was all right, and called Sancho to pacify him. He was just putting his little hand on the dog's neck and beginning to smile through his tears, when I heard, behind me, a click of the iron gate, and the rustle of female garments, and lo! Mrs. Graham darted upon me—her neck uncovered, her black locks streaming in the wind.

'Give me the child!' she said, in a voice scarce louder than a whisper, but with a tone of startling vehemence, and, seizing the boy, she snatched him from me, as if some dire contamination were in my touch, and then stood with one hand firmly clasping his, the other on his shoulder, fixing upon me her large, luminous, dark eyes—pale, breathless, quivering with agitation.

'I was not harming the child, madam,' said I, scarce knowing whether to be most astonished or displeased; 'he was tumbling off the wall there; and I was so fortunate as to catch him, while he hung suspended headlong from that tree, and prevent I know not what catastrophe.'

'I beg your pardon, sir,' stammered she; suddenly calming down,—the light of reason seeming to break upon her beclouded spirit, and a faint blush mantling on her cheek —'I did not know you;—and I thought—'

She stooped to kiss the child, and fondly clasped her arm round his neck.

'You thought I was going to kidnap your son, I suppose?'

The Tenant of Wildfell Hall, ch. 2

Before comparing the styles of Emily and Anne it is necessary to see what Anne was doing, and how it differs from Emily's approach. In Emily's mind, the whole novel exists in entirety at once, and each part reflects, forwards and backwards, on the whole. Anne uses a simpler method of expansion, developing the novel step by step in the usual way—but not without subtlety. Note how she stresses, without seeming to, the faded elegance of Wildfell Hall. Again, consider the various ways in which she arouses interest in the lady (who has already been mentioned as a rather mysterious recluse, earlier in the book), and the impression Anne creates of her when she appears. Her sudden appearance is important, of course, as is the fact that she is the first person of interest to appear—otherwise we have only the colourless narrator, a dog, and a child. Turning from her, it is also valuable to study the narrative skill shown here—how Anne Brontë arouses interest and creates movement. Then a comparison with extracts 1 and 4 may be attempted, beginning perhaps with the question: 'How do the two sisters contrive to infuse emotion into description?'

The character of 'Wuthering Heights'

After the chilly meal described in extract 4, Lockwood finds himself snowed into the farmhouse for the night and, unknown to Heathcliff, he is put in a barely furnished bedroom: 'the whole furniture consisted of a chair, a clothes-press, and a large oak case', which turns out to be the bed, built in against a window and enclosed with wooden panels. There he finds the carved name of Catherine *Earnshaw* or *Linton* or *Heathcliff* (i.e., Cathy, long-dead mother of the Catherine of the earlier extracts; born Catherine Earnshaw, becoming Linton by marriage, but never Heathcliff except in her imagination). He picks up and reads an old mildewed book whose margins were her childhood diary. When Lockwood drops off to sleep, his reading forms the material of two dreams, described in this extract.

They are dreams; yet they display the character of the novel—grotesqueness, violence and mystery, especially the mystery of the dream-figure of Cathy—deepened by the unexpected reaction of Heathcliff. Emily Brontë always ensures that the apparently supernatural features of her narrative can be given a rational explanation. She does not depend on 'magic' and its meretricious effects. Lockwood

42

has read in the 'diary', and seen about him, sufficient material for his dream; and the incidents, as may be expected, form no part of the plot. But these dreams are the imaginative core of the novel—the image of the intractable Heathcliff haunted and dominated by the unattainable Cathy. There is no ghost; only a branch tapping on a window. Yet Lockwood, in his own awkward manner, has come to the centre of the situation: for Heathcliff *is* haunted.

Among the images of the passage, not the least important are those of the window-bed and of Gimmerton chapel. These will form part of the substance of another extract—no. 10: at present they may simply be noticed.

6

I began to nod drowsily over the dim page; my eye wandered from manuscript to print. I saw a red ornamented title[1] . . . 'Seventy Times Seven, and the First of the Seventy First. A Pious Discourse delivered by the Reverend Jabes Branderham, in the Chapel of Gimmerden Sough.' And while I was, half-consciously, worrying my brain to guess what Jabes Branderham would make of his subject, I sank back in bed, and fell asleep.

Alas, for the effects of bad tea and bad temper! what else could it be that made me pass such a terrible night? I don't remember another that I can at all compare with it since I was capable of suffering.

I began to dream, almost before I ceased to be sensible of my locality. I thought it was morning; and I had set out on my way home, with Joseph for a guide. The snow lay yards deep in our road; and, as we floundered on, my companion wearied me with constant reproaches that I had not brought a pilgrim's staff: telling me that I could never get into the house without one, and boastfully flourishing a heavy-headed cudgel, which I understood to be so denominated.

For a moment I considered it absurd that I should need such a weapon to gain admittance into my own residence. Then, a new idea flashed across me. I was not going there; we were journeying to hear the famous Jabes Branderham preach from the text—'Seventy Times Seven'; and either Joseph, the preacher, or I had committed the 'First of the Seventy First,' and were to be publicly exposed and excommunicated.

We came to the chapel—I have passed it really in my walks, twice or thrice: it lies in a hollow, between two hills—an elevated hollow—near a swamp, whose peaty moisture is said to answer all the purposes of embalming on the few corpses deposited there. The roof has been kept whole hitherto but, as the clergyman's stipend is only twenty pounds per annum, and a house with two rooms, threatening speedily to determine into one, no clergyman will undertake the duties of pastor, especially as it is currently reported that his flock would rather let him starve than increase the living by one penny from their own pockets. However, in my dream, Jabes had a full and attentive congregation: and he preached—good God —what a sermon! divided into *four hundred and ninety* parts—each fully equal to an ordinary address from the pulpit—and each discussing a separate sin! Where he searched for them, I cannot tell; he had his private manner of interpreting the phrase, and it seemed necessary the brother should sin different sins on every occasion.

They were of the most curious character—odd transgressions that I never imagined previously.

Oh, how weary I grew. How I writhed, and yawned,

and nodded, and revived! How I pinched and pricked myself, and rubbed my eyes, and stood up, and sat down again, and nudged Joseph to inform me if he would *ever* have done!

I was condemned to hear all out—finally, he reached the *'First of the Seventy First.'* At that crisis, a sudden inspiration descended on me; I was moved to rise and denounce Jabes Branderham as the sinner of the sin that no christian need pardon.

'Sir,' I exclaimed, 'sitting here within these four walls, at one stretch, I have endured and forgiven the four hundred and ninety heads of your discourse. Seventy times seven times have I plucked up my hat, and been about to depart —Seventy times seven times have you preposterously forced me to resume my seat. The four hundred and ninety-first is too much. Fellow martyrs, have at him! Drag him down, and crush him to atoms, that the place which knows him may know him no more!'

'*Thou art the Man!*' cried Jabes, after a solemn pause, leaning over his cushion. 'Seventy times seven didst thou gapingly contort thy visage—seventy times seven did I take counsel with my soul—Lo, this is human weakness; this also may be absolved! The First of the Seventy First is come. Brethren, execute upon him the judgment written! such honour have all His saints!'

With that concluding word, the whole assembly, exalting their pilgrim's staves, rushed round me in a body, and I, having no weapon to raise in self-defence, commenced grappling with Joseph, my nearest and most ferocious assailant, for his. In the confluence of the multitude, several clubs crossed; blows, aimed at me, fell on other sconces. Presently the whole chapel resounded with rappings and counter-rappings. Every man's hand was against his neighbour; and Branderham, unwilling to remain idle, poured forth his zeal in a shower of loud taps on the boards of the pulpit which resounded so smartly that, at last, to my unspeakable relief, they woke me.

And what was it that had suggested the tremendous tumult, what had played Jabes' part in the row? Merely, the branch of a fir-tree that touched my lattice, as the blast wailed by, and rattled its dry cones against the panes!

I listened doubtingly an instant; detected the disturber, then turned and dozed, and dreamt again; if possible, still more disagreeably than before.

This time, I remembered I was lying in the oak closet, and I heard distinctly the gusty wind, and the driving of the snow; I heard, also, the fir bough repeat its teasing sound, and ascribed it to the right cause: but, it annoyed me so much, that I resolved to silence it, if possible; and, I thought, I rose and endeavoured to unhasp the casement. The hook was soldered into the staple, a circumstance observed by me, when awake, but forgotten.

'I must stop it, nevertheless!' I muttered, knocking my knuckles through the glass, and stretching an arm out to seize the importunate branch: instead of which, my fingers closed on the fingers of a little, ice-cold hand!

The intense horror of nightmare came over me; I tried to draw back my arm, but the hand clung to it, and a most melancholy voice sobbed,

'Let me in—let me in!'

'Who are you?' I asked struggling, meanwhile, to disengage myself.

'Catherine Linton,' it replied shiveringly (why did I think of *Linton*? I had read *Earnshaw* twenty times for Linton), 'I'm come home, I'd lost my way on the moor!'

As it spoke, I discerned, obscurely, a child's face looking through the window—Terror made me cruel; and, finding it useless to attempt shaking the creature off, I pulled its wrist on to the broken pane, and rubbed it to and fro till the blood ran down and soaked the bed-clothes: still it wailed, 'Let me in!' and maintained its tenacious gripe, almost maddening me with fear.

'How can I!' I said at length. 'Let *me* go, if you want me to let you in!'

The fingers relaxed, I snatched mine through the hole, hurriedly piled the books up in a pyramid against it, and stopped my ears to exclude the lamentable prayer.

I seemed to keep them closed above a quarter of an hour, yet, the instant I listened, again, there was the doleful cry moaning on!

'Begone!' I shouted, 'I'll never let you in, not if you beg for twenty years!'

'It's twenty years,' mourned the voice, 'twenty years, I've been a waif for twenty years!'

Thereat began a feeble scratching outside, and the pile of books moved as if thrust forward.

I tried to jump up; but could not stir a limb; and so yelled aloud, in a frenzy of fright.

To my confusion, I discovered the yell was not ideal[2]. Hasty footsteps approached my chamber door: somebody pushed it open, with a vigorous hand, and a light glimmered through the squares at the top of the bed. I sat shuddering, yet, and wiping the perspiration from my forehead: the intruder appeared to hesitate and muttered to himself.

At last, he said in a half-whisper, plainly not expecting an answer,

'Is any one here?'

I considered it best to confess my presence, for I knew Heathcliff's accents, and feared he might search further, if I kept quiet.

With this intention, I turned and opened the panels— I shall not soon forget the effect my action produced.

Heathcliff stood near the entrance, in his shirt and

trousers; with a candle dripping over his fingers, and his face as white as the wall behind him. The first creak of the oak startled him like an electric shock: the light leaped from his hold to a distance of some feet, and his agitation was so extreme that he could hardly pick it up.

Wuthering Heights, ch. 3

Notes
  [1] *a title*: of a genuine (not dreamt) book of sermons.
  [2] *ideal*: existing in the realm of ideas, not of phenomena.

Such a word as *character* applied to a novel is dangerous, since it sounds well but may have no more than a vague substitute for meaning. As used here, it refers to the distinctive flavour of the novel, caused by a particular blending of many ingredients, with a result that is quite different from the novels of other writers. The reader can only verify this for himself when he has read the novel through, and enough other novels besides to be able to make a comparison. However, something of it can already be detected here. Emily Brontë uses various devices to induce the sense of dreaming—some for plausibility, some for atmosphere. These are worth studying for their own sake. But she goes on to use the inconsequentiality of dreams for her own purposes. The first dream is grotesque and comic, but it is necessary for both contrast and atmosphere. The nature of the comedy, with the sophisticated Lockwood in a brawl in a country chapel is significant. It is only half-amusing; it is almost macabre, and so by contrast and parallel we move into the second dream. Several parallels may be explored; the violence

48

of the two scenes—in the first, it gets Lockwood out of difficulty, but in the second it does him no good. Or the imagery of moors and darkness in both—to what extent does it cohere into a cumulative whole, and to what extent is it treated differently?

Emily Bronte's narrative method

Many of the main features of Emily Brontë's narrative are illustrated in this extract. Nelly Dean is telling the story, and has come to a critical point—the return of Heathcliff after a long and unexplained absence. She pauses, therefore, for a moment's comment before passing on to the event itself. The comment is foreboding, and the passage repeatedly shows the writer's use of suspense. The reader must have guessed almost at once that the mysterious stranger is Heathcliff; yet she does not tell us so, holding off from one paragraph to another until at last he announces himself. Secondly, note her use of contrast. Nelly, having ended her comments, describes a beautiful evening—and puts the dark figure of Heathcliff in the midst of it. Later, she describes the peace of the household—and breaks it for ever by Cathy's excitement and Heathcliff's entry. Thirdly, her use of implicit as well as explicit statement. Although she has prepared us for an ominous change, she uses indirect hints only: she at no point says explicitly that Heathcliff has come to work destruction (as we later discover he has). The foreboding lies entirely in the dark, almost silent, enigmatic figure of the man, recognised yet a stranger, named but unknown. The effect of his arrival is seen in the others, not through any action of his. Nelly is disquieted, Linton is somewhat put out, Cathy is wildly delighted; Heathcliff is cool. Yet—another typical feature—what little he does say shows the hidden fires that are burning: he cannot stay away from Cathy. This is the constant element of the story, which provides its motive power. Finally, note the mention of the view from the Grange, over Gimmerton and towards the Heights—in itself of no importance, yet these are places which recur and—with the images of bed and window shown in the previous extract—form a background of inanimate things in front of which the human story is worked out.

7

On a mellow evening in September, I was coming from the garden with a heavy basket of apples which I had been gathering. It had got dusk, and the moon looked over the high wall of the court, causing undefined shadows to lurk in the corners of the numerous projecting portions of the building. I set my burden on the house steps by the kitchen door, and lingered to rest, and drew in a few more breaths of the soft, sweet air; my eyes were on the moon, and my back to the entrance, when I heard a voice behind me say—

'Nelly, is that you?'

It was a deep voice, and foreign in tone; yet, there was something in the manner of pronouncing my name which made it sound familiar. I turned about to discover who spoke, fearfully, for the doors were shut, and I had seen nobody on approaching the steps.

Something stirred in the porch; and moving nearer, I distinguished a tall man dressed in dark clothes, with dark face and hair. He leant against the side, and held his fingers on the latch, as if intending to open for himself.

'Who can it be?' I thought. 'Mr. Earnshaw, Oh, no! The voice has no resemblance to his.'

'I have waited here an hour,' he resumed, while I continued staring; 'and the whole of that time all round has been as still as death. I dared not enter. You do not know me? Look, I'm not a stranger!'

A ray fell on his features; the cheeks were sallow, and half covered with black whiskers; the brows lowering, the eyes deep set and singular. I remembered the eyes.

'What!' I cried, uncertain whether to regard him as a worldly visitor, and I raised my hands in amazement. 'What! you come back? Is it really you? Is it?'

'Yes, Heathcliff,' he replied, glancing from me up to the windows which reflected a score of glittering moons, but showed no lights from within. 'Are they at home—where is she? Nelly, you are not glad—you needn't be so disturbed. Is she here? Speak! I wait to have one word with her—your mistress. Go, and say some person from Gimmerton desires to see her.'

'How will she take it?' I exclaimed. 'What will she do? The surprise bewilders me—it will put her out of her head! And you *are* Heathcliff? But altered! Nay, there's no comprehending it. Have you been for a soldier?'

'Go, and carry my message,' he interrupted impatiently; 'I'm in hell till you do!'

He lifted the latch, and I entered; but when I got to the parlour where Mr. and Mrs. Linton were, I could not persuade myself to proceed.

At length, I resolved on making an excuse to ask if they would have the candles lighted, and I opened the door.

They sat together in a window whose lattice lay back against the wall, and displayed, beyond the garden trees and the wild green park, the valley of Gimmerton, with a long line of mist winding nearly to its top (for very soon after you pass the chapel, as you may have noticed, the sough that runs from the marshes joins a beck which follows the bend of the glen), Wuthering Heights rose above this silvery vapour—but our old house was invisible —it rather dips down on the other side.

Both the room, and its occupants, and the scene they gazed on, looked wondrously peaceful. I shrank reluctantly from performing my errand: and was actually going away, leaving it unsaid, after having put my question about the candles, when a sense of my folly compelled me to return, and mutter:

'A person from Gimmerton wishes to see you, ma'am.'

'What does he want?' asked Mrs. Linton.

'I did not question him,' I answered.

'Well, close the curtains, Nelly,' she said; 'and bring up tea. I'll be back again directly.'

She quitted the apartment; Mr. Edgar inquired, carelessly, who it was.

'Some one mistress does not expect,' I replied. 'That Heathcliff, you recollect him, sir, who used to live at Mr. Earnshaw's.'

'What, the gipsy—the plough-boy?' he cried. 'Why did you not say so to Catherine?'

'Hush! you must not call him by those names, master,' I said. 'She'd be sadly grieved to hear you. She was nearly heartbroken when he ran off; I guess his return will make a jubilee to her.'

Mr. Linton walked to a window on the other side of the room that overlooked the court. He unfastened it, and leant out. I suppose they were below, for he exclaimed, quickly:

'Don't stand there, love! Bring the person in, if it be any one particular.'

Ere long, I heard the click of the latch, and Catherine flew upstairs, breathless and wild, too excited to show gladness; indeed, by her face, you would rather have surmised an awful calamity.

'Oh, Edgar, Edgar!' she panted, flinging her arms round his neck. 'Oh, Edgar, darling! Heathcliff's come back—he is!' And she tightened her embrace to a squeeze.

'Well, well,' cried her husband, crossly, 'don't strangle me for that! He never struck me as such a marvellous treasure. There is no need to be frantic!'

'I know you didn't like him,' she answered, repressing a little the intensity of her delight. 'Yet, for my sake, you must be friends now. Shall I tell him to come up now?'

'Here?' he said, 'into the parlour?'

'Where else?' she asked.

He looked vexed, and suggested the kitchen as a more suitable place for him.

Mrs. Linton eyed him with a droll expression—half angry, half laughing at his fastidiousness.

'No,' she added, after a while: 'I cannot sit in the kitchen. Set two tables here, Ellen; one for your master and Miss Isabella, being gentry; the other for Heathcliff and myself, being of the lower orders. Will that please you, dear? Or must I have a fire lighted elsewhere? If so, give directions. I'll run down and secure my guest. I'm afraid the joy is too great to be real!'

She was about to dart off again; but Edgar arrested her.

'You bid him step up,' he said, addressing me; 'and Catherine, try to be glad, without being absurd. The whole household need not witness the sight of your welcoming a runaway servant as a brother.'

I descended and found Heathcliff waiting under the porch, evidently anticipating an invitation to enter. He followed my guidance without waste of words, and I ushered him into the presence of the master and mistress, whose flushed cheeks betrayed signs of warm talking. But the lady's glowed with another feeling when her friend appeared at the door; she sprang forward, took both his hands, and led him to Linton; and then she seized Linton's reluctant fingers and crushed them into his.

Now fully revealed by the fire and candlelight, I was amazed, more than ever, to behold the transformation of Heathcliff. He had grown a tall, athletic, well-formed man, beside whom, my master seemed quite slender and youth-like. His upright carriage suggested the idea of his having been in the army. His countenance was much older in expression and decision of feature than Mr. Linton's; it looked intelligent, and retained no marks of former de-gradation. A half-civilised ferocity lurked yet in the depressed brows, and eyes full of black fire, but it was subdued; and his manner was even dignified, quite divested of roughness though too stern for grace.

My master's surprise equalled or exceeded mine: he remained for a minute at a loss how to address the plough-boy, as he had called him, Heathcliff dropped his slight hand, and stood looking at him coolly till he chose to speak.

Wuthering Heights, ch. 10

The use of visual and other narrative techniques as in-dicated in the headnote should be given a careful study; and since the headnote does not claim to be exhaustive, the reader will probably find others. There are two sides to such a study—to detect the effects aimed at, and the methods by which they are achieved. It is also interesting to see how much information is imparted along with the narration of events. For example, Heathcliff is a central figure; but what do we *know* of him from this passage?

(and in what senses of the word *know*?). By contrast, consider the use of the bystander Nelly—the degree to which her character is produced, and yet how far it is subdued to the author's other interests. Again, the effect of momentary actions and words or comments should be considered, as a change from the study of carefully-assembled effects. An example of this is Nelly's remark of Cathy—'. . . by her face, you would rather have surmised an awful calamity'. This tells us a great deal, in a moment, about Cathy and about the story.

The violence of 'Wuthering Heights'

Wherever Heathcliff is, violence erupts. Often it is his own; sometimes, as here, it is the violence of others which bursts out at his presence. Heathcliff, on his return (described in the previous extract) deliberately provokes his foster-brother Hindley into excesses of drinking and gambling (with Heathcliff the winner) so as to get the Heights into his own hands. Then he makes a runaway marriage with Isabella Linton, Cathy's sister-in-law, and on his return to the Heights makes her life such a misery that in the end she runs away. (This is an act, in Victorian eyes, tantamount to infidelity, and only justified by the most intolerable circumstances—as in Anne Brontë's *Wildfell Hall*, which also describes a foolish marriage and a runaway wife.)

This extract is part of Isabella's story, which she tells to Nelly when she gets to Thrushcross Grange, where she stops only briefly (so as to avoid her estranged brother); but long enough to narrate the events of her marriage. The immediate cause of her escape was the quarrel here, following a night of terror when Heathcliff returned home after staying out past midnight at Cathy's grave (she had been buried the previous day). Hindley had waited up for him, threatening to shoot him; but Heathcliff over-powered Hindley and retaliated brutally. The gratuitous violence of her story may seem implausible out of context, although it is only the milder half of a narrative that twice includes near-murder. Yet, with the novel half-completed, it has become typical of Heathcliff's sur-roundings: wherever he is, people show their most savage nature. For all that, Nelly retells it as if it were a story of the most prosaic kind—note her ready moral inter-jection, and most of all, the last sentence of the extract.

8

'This morning, when I came down, about half-an-hour before noon, Mr. Earnshaw[1] was sitting by the fire, deadly sick; his evil genius[2] almost as gaunt and ghastly, leant against the chimney. Neither appeared inclined to dine; and, having waited till all was cold on the table, I com-menced alone.

'Nothing hindered me from eating heartily; and I ex-perienced a certain sense of satisfaction and superiority, as, at intervals, I cast a look towards my silent companions, and felt the comfort of a quiet conscience within me.

'After I had done, I ventured on the unusual liberty of drawing near the fire, going round Earnshaw's seat, and kneeling in the corner beside him.

'Heathcliff did not glance my way and I gazed up and contemplated his features, almost as confidently as if they had been turned to stone. His forehead, that I once thought so manly, and that I now think so diabolical, was shaded with a heavy cloud; his basilisk eyes were nearly quenched by sleeplessness—and weeping, perhaps, for the lashes were wet then; his lips devoid of their ferocious sneer, and sealed in an expression of unspeakable sadness. Had it been another, I would have covered my face, in the presence of such grief. In *his* case, I was gratified, and ignoble as it seems to insult a fallen enemy, I couldn't miss this chance of sticking in a dart; his weakness was the only time when I could taste the delight of paying wrong for wrong.'

'Fie, fie, Miss!' I interrupted. 'One might suppose you had never opened a Bible in your life. If God afflict your enemies, surely that ought to suffice you. It is both mean and presumptuous to add your torture to his!'

'In general, I'll allow that it would be, Ellen,' she continued. 'But what misery laid on Heathcliff would content me, unless I have a hand in it? I'd rather he suffered *less*, if I might cause his sufferings, and he might *know* that I was the cause. Oh, I owe him so much. On only one condition can I hope to forgive him. It is, if I may take an eye for an eye, a tooth for a tooth, for every wrench of agony, return a wrench, reduce him to my level. As he was the first to injure, make him the first to implore pardon; and then—why then, Ellen, I might show you some generosity. But it is utterly impossible I can ever be revenged, and therefore I cannot forgive him. Hindley wanted some water, and I handed him a glass, and asked him how he was.

' "Not as ill as I wish," he replied. "But leaving out my arm, every inch of me is as sore as if I had been fighting with a legion of imps!"

' "Yes, no wonder," was my next remark. "Catherine used to boast that she stood between you and bodily harm—she meant that certain persons would not hurt you, for fear of offending her. It's well people don't *really* rise from their grave, or, last night, she might have witnessed a repulsive scene! Are not you bruised, and cut over your chest and shoulders?"

' "I can't say," he answered; "but what do you mean? Did he dare to strike me when I was down?"

' "He trampled on, and kicked you, and dashed you on the ground," I whispered. "And his mouth watered to tear you with his teeth; because, he's only half a man—not so much."

'Mr. Earnshaw looked up, like me, to the countenance of our mutual foe; who, absorbed in his anguish, seemed insensible to anything around him; the longer he stood, the plainer his reflections revealed their blackness through his features.

' "Oh, if God would but give me strength to strangle him in my last agony, I'd go to hell with joy," groaned the impatient man, writhing to rise, and sinking back in despair, convinced of his inadequacy for the struggle.

' "Nay, it's enough that he has murdered one of you," I observed aloud. "At the Grange, every one knows your sister would have been living now, had it not been for Mr. Heathcliff. After all, it is preferable to be hated than loved by him. When I recollect how happy we were— how happy Catherine was before he came—I'm fit to curse the day."

'Most likely, Heathcliff noticed more the truth of what was said, than the spirit of the person who said it. His attention was roused, I saw, for his eyes rained down tears among the ashes, and he drew his breath in suffocating sighs.

'I stared full at him, and laughed scornfully. The clouded windows of hell flashed a moment towards me; the fiend which usually looked out, however, was so dimmed and drowned that I did not fear to hazard another sound of derision.

' "Get up, and begone out of my sight," said the mourner.

'I guessed he uttered those words, at least, though his voice was hardly intelligible.

'"I beg your pardon," I replied. "But I loved Catherine, too; and her brother requires attendance which, for her sake, I shall supply. Now that she's dead, I see her in Hindley; Hindley has exactly her eyes, if you had not tried to gouge them out, and made them black and red, and her—"

'"Get up, wretched idiot, before I stamp you to death!" he cried, making a movement that caused me to make one also.

'"But then," I continued, holding myself ready to flee; "if poor Catherine had trusted you, and assumed the ridiculous, contemptible, degrading title of Mrs. Heathcliff, she would soon have presented a similar picture! *She* wouldn't have borne your abominable behaviour quietly; her detestation and disgust must have found voice."

'The back of the settle and Earnshaw's person interposed between me and him; so instead of endeavouring to reach me he snatched a dinner knife from the table, and flung it at my head. It struck beneath my ear[3], and stopped the sentence I was uttering; but pulling it out, I sprang to the door, and delivered another which I hope went a little deeper than his missile.

'The last glimpse I caught of him was a furious rush on his part, checked by the embrace of his host; and both fell locked together on the hearth.

'In my flight through the kitchen, I bid Joseph speed to his master; I knocked over Hareton[4], who was hanging a litter of puppies from a chairback in the doorway; and, blest as a soul escaped from purgatory, I bounded, leaped, and flew down the steep road: then, quitting its windings, shot direct across the moor, rolling over banks, and wading through marshes; precipitating myself, in fact, towards the beacon light of the Grange. And far rather would

I be condemned to a perpetual dwelling in the infernal regions, than even for one night abide beneath the roof of Wuthering Heights again.'

Isabella ceased speaking, and took a drink of tea . . .

Wuthering Heights, ch. 17

Notes
[1] *Mr. Earnshaw* : Hindley, Cathy's brother.
[2] *his evil genius* : Heathcliff.
[3] *It struck beneath my ear* : On Isabella's arrival, Nelly recalls that 'there was a deep cut under one ear, which only the cold prevented from bleeding profusely.'
[4] *Hareton* : At this time a child of five.

The violence of this passage shows most obviously in Heathcliff, and to some extent in Hindley. But Isabella herself contributes to it, and it is worth while examining her character in this light, as it is shown here. In the scene a variety of means are used, of which personality is only one, to depict the violence which is the rule in Wuthering Heights, and to make it appear intolerable. Even such slight matters as Nelly's interruption, and the various references to food and drink, have their place.

Moralising in 'Wildfell Hall'

As will be seen, such pointing of opinion—scarcely moralising—as there is in *Agnes Grey* is very gentle. It is surprising for the modern reader to be told that *Wildfell Hall* was received with much moral disapproval, and difficult at first sight to see where this could fall. As a later extract (no. 14) shows, the heroine is too much given to moralising herself, and this, rather than the opposite fault, is likely to strike the twentieth-century reader. In fact, Anne Brontë wrote the book largely as an unpleasant duty, to depict the ugliness of the drunkard's fate—as she had seen it overtake her own brother—and, unlike many other writers, she was not content to generalise about 'the evils of drink', but showed the victim himself vacillating between bravado and regret, brave resolution and weak surrender, finally dying in terror. The following extract illustrates both features of the novel—which displease the prejudices of one age or the other, but which give the novel its character. Arthur Huntingdon is dangerously ill, and as a result his cynical self-centredness is to the fore. Helen is more sympathetic than she had been, but still given—too much so for most modern tastes—to theologising. Yet even this would not necessarily please the reader of 1850, for her 'preaching' is slightly untraditional. It is not of condemnation, but of purification—she does not treat the drunkard as an outcast, but as unhappy. Helen Huntingdon has learnt more tolerance, though she has not changed her principles.

9

The first of these communications brought intelligence of a serious relapse in Mr. Huntingdon's illness, entirely the result of his own infatuation in persisting in the indulgence of his appetite for stimulating drink. In vain had she remonstrated, in vain she had mingled his wine with water: her arguments and entreaties were a nuisance, her interference was an insult so intolerable, that, at length, on finding she had covertly diluted the pale port that was brought him, he threw the bottle out of the window, swearing he would not be cheated like a baby, ordered the butler, on pain of instant dismissal, to bring a bottle of the strongest wine in the cellar, and affirming that he should have been well long ago if he had been let to have his own way, but she wanted to keep him weak in order that she might have him under her thumb —but by the Lord Harry, he would have no more humbug—seized a glass in one hand and a bottle in the other, and never rested till he had drunk it dry. Alarming symptoms were the immediate result of this 'Imprudence', as she mildly termed it—symptoms which had rather increased than diminished since; and this was the cause of her delay in writing to her brother. Every former feature of his malady had returned with augmented virulence: the slight external wound, inflammation had taken place, which might terminate fatally if not soon removed. Of course, the wretched sufferer's temper was not improved by this calamity—in fact, I suspect it was well nigh insupportable, though his kind nurse did not complain; but she said she had been obliged at last to give her son in charge to Esther Hargrave, as her presence was so constantly required in the sickroom that she could not possibly attend to him herself; and though the child had begged to be allowed to continue with her there, and to help her to nurse his papa, and though she had no doubt he would have been very good and quiet,—she could not think of subjecting his young and tender feelings to the sight of so much suffering, or of allowing him to witness his father's impatience, or hear the dreadful language he was wont to use in his paroxysms of pain or irritation.

'The latter,' continued she, 'most deeply regrets the step that has occasioned his relapse,—but, as usual, he throws the blame upon me. If I had reasoned with him like a rational creature, he says, it never would have happened; but to be treated like a baby or a fool, was enough to put any man past his patience, and drive him to assert his independence even at the sacrifice of his own interest— he forgets how often I had reasoned him "past his patience" before. He appears to be sensible of his danger; but nothing can induce him to behold it in the proper light. The other night while I was waiting on him, and just as I had brought him a draught to assuage his burning thirst—he observed, with a return of his former sarcastic bitterness,—

'Yes, you're mighty attentive now!—I suppose there's nothing you wouldn't do for me now?'

'You know,' said I, a little surprised at his manner, 'that I am willing to do anything I can to relieve you.'

'Yes, now, my immaculate angel; but when once you have secured your reward, and find yourself safe in heaven, and me howling in hell-fire, catch you lifting a finger to serve me then!—No, you'll look complacently on, and not so much as dip the tip of your finger in water to cool my tongue!'

'If so, it will be because of the great gulf over which I cannot pass; and if I could look complacently on in such a case, it would be only from the assurance that you were being purified from your sins, and fitted to enjoy the happiness I felt.—But are you determined, Arthur, that I shall not meet you in heaven?'

'Humph! What should I do there, I should like to know?'

'Indeed, I cannot tell; and I fear it is too certain that your tastes and feelings must be widely altered before you can have any enjoyment there.'

'But do you prefer sinking, without an effort, into the state of torment you picture to yourself?'

'Oh, it's all a fable,' said he contemptuously.

'Are you sure, Arthur? are you quite sure? Because if there is any doubt, and if you should find yourself mistaken after all, when it is too late to turn—'

'It would be rather awkward, to be sure,' said he; 'but don't bother me now—I'm not going to die yet. I can't and won't,' he added vehemently, as if suddenly struck with the appalling aspect of that terrible event. 'Helen, you must save me!' And he earnestly seized my hand, and looked into my face with such imploring eagerness that my heart bled for him, and I could not speak for tears.

The Tenant of Wildfell Hall, ch. 49

This passage is not immediately acceptable to the modern reader, who is conditioned to object to simple and strong demonstrations of moral and religious beliefs, and to certain other features of the episode. It is important for us, first, to appreciate the ideas of other ages on their own grounds; and second, to accept that perhaps we may be no more right than they were. Then we can consider the passage with a much greater probability of real understanding. One may compare the religious attitudes of Emily and Anne Brontë, which are fairly well exemplified in the extracts in this book. The two sisters may well turn out to be much less at variance than at first appears. Religious attitudes are essentially different from moral attitudes, though they are commonly confused.

From a more literary point of view, certain parallels appear between this and extract 8. Both passages have a certain apparent implausibility—we might say that the speeches are high-flown, and that this makes the characters seem larger and more rigid than life. This question is discussed in the following extracts; for the present it may be observed that this larger-than-life, dramatic quality is essential to many novels of the period, and the student might consider this quality in the extracts he has already read, and note its virtues and uses rather than its defects.

Speech in 'Wuthering Heights'

A novelist uses conversation for two purposes—to advance the action, and to display the character of the speaker. In both cases, speech has the advantage of being *direct*; the writer is not describing or explaining, but actually demonstrating the personality of the speaker in action. Nevertheless, the tradition of completely realistic dialogue took a long time to grow. Much of the conversation in novels of the eighteenth and nineteenth centuries is written in a composed style such as the most formal of talkers is unlikely ever to have used. This tradition was still active in the Brontës' time; such artificial speech may be found on the lips of characters in Dickens and Thackeray, for example. It is a mistake to criticise this kind of speech for its artificiality; it is not meant to be 'real'. When necessary, the writer will turn to a more natural mode of speech; but in places where the action demands a heightened atmosphere, concentration of purpose, or merely thorough exposition, the writer controls the speaker's words so that they convey character through the action spoken of, rather than through the speech : and not only the character of the speaker, but also the author's interpretation of his words. Just so, the Elizabethan dramatists made their characters love and die in blank verse. So also the modern detective novelist almost inevitably writes a last chapter containing a speech of lengthy explanation such as no detective would ever really make.

The following extracts show the variety of speech in *Wuthering Heights*, from Joseph's broad dialect to Heathcliff's self-revelation. Note that only Joseph, and not his fellow-servants, is represented semi-phonetically— Zillah, for example, would speak just like him. There is no clear boundary between realism and formalism; these pieces show how they may shade into one another. This is part of an interview which takes place shortly after Heathcliff has returned to the Heights, after his runaway marriage with Isabella. Nelly has come to the Heights and found them both in: Heathcliff is speaking.

10

'Tell your master, Nelly, that I never, in all my life, met with such an abject thing as she is—She even disgraces the name of Linton; and I've sometimes relented, from pure lack of invention, in my experiments on what she could endure, and still creep shamefully cringing back! But tell him also, to set his fraternal and magisterial heart at ease, that I keep strictly within the limits of the law—I have avoided, up to this period, giving her the slightest right to claim a separation; and what's more, she'd thank nobody for dividing us—if she desired to go she might—the nuisance of her presence outweighs the gratification to be derived from tormenting her!'

'Mr. Heathcliff,' said I, 'this is the talk of a madman, and your wife, most likely, is convinced you are mad; and, for that reason, she has borne with you hitherto: but now that you say she may go, she'll doubtless avail herself of the permission—You are not so bewitched, ma'am, are you, as to remain with him, of your own accord?'

'Take care, Ellen!' answered Isabella, her eyes sparkling irefully—there was no misdoubting by their expression, the full success of her partner's endeavours to make himself detested. 'Don't put faith in a single word he speaks. He's a lying fiend, a monster, and not a human being! I've been told I might leave him before; and I've made the attempt, but I dare not repeat it! Only, Ellen, promise you'll not mention a syllable of his infamous conversation to my brother or Catherine[1]—whatever he may pretend, he wishes to provoke Edgar to desperation—he says he has married me on purpose to obtain power over him; and he shan't obtain it—I'll die first! I just hope, I pray that he may forget his diabolical prudence, and kill me! The single pleasure I can imagine is to die, or to see him dead!'

'There—that will do for the present!' said Heathcliff. 'If you are called upon in a court of law, you'll remember her language, Nelly! And take a good look at that countenance—she's near the point which would suit me. No, you're not fit to be your own guardian, Isabella, now; and I, being your legal protector, must retain you in my custody, however distasteful the obligation may be— Go upstairs; I have something to say to Ellen Dean, in private. That's not the way—upstairs, I tell you! Why, this is the road upstairs, child!'

He seized, and thrust her from the room; and returned muttering,

'I have no pity! I have no pity! The more the worms writhe, the more I yearn to crush out their entrails! It is a moral teething, and I grind with greater energy, in proportion to the increase of pain.'

'Do you understand what the word pity means?' I said, hastening to resume my bonnet. 'Did you ever feel a touch of it in your life?'

'Put that down!' he interrupted, perceiving my intention to depart. 'You are not going yet—Come here now, Nelly—I must either persuade, or compel you to aid me in fulfilling my determination to see Catherine, and that without delay—I swear that I meditate no harm; I don't desire to cause any disturbance, or to exasperate, or insult Mr. Linton; I only wish to hear from herself how she is, and why she has been ill; and to ask, if anything that I could do would be of use to her. Last night, I was in the Grange garden six hours, and I'll return there to-night; and every night I'll haunt the place, and every day, till I find an opportunity of entering. If Edgar Linton meets me, I shall not hesitate to knock him down, and give him enough to ensure his quiescence while I stay—If his servants oppose me, I shall threaten them off with these pistols—But wouldn't it be better to prevent my coming in contact with them, or their master? And you could do it so easily! I'd warn you when I came, and then you might let me in unobserved, as soon as she was alone, and watch till I departed—your conscience quite calm, you would be hindering mischief.'

I protested against playing that treacherous part in my employer's house; and besides, I urged the cruelty and selfishness, of his destroying Mrs. Linton's tranquillity, for his satisfaction.

'The commonest occurrence startles her painfully,' I said. 'She's all nerves, and she couldn't bear the surprise, I'm positive—Don't persist, sir! or else, I shall be obliged to inform my master of your designs, and he'll take measures to secure his house and its inmates from any such unwarrantable intrusions!'

'In that case, I'll take measures to secure you, woman!'

exclaimed Heathcliff, 'you shall not leave Wuthering
Heights till to-morrow morning.'

Wuthering Heights, ch. 14

*

This describes the younger Catherine's first appearance
downstairs after recovering from the death of her boy-
husband Linton. Zillah speaks.

11

'Joseph and I generally go to chapel on Sundays,' (the
Kirk[2], you know, has no minister, now, explained Mrs.
Dean; and they call the Methodists' or Baptists' place, I
can't say which it is, at Gimmerton, a chapel). 'Joseph
had gone,' she continued, 'but I thought proper to bide
at home. Young folks are always the better for an elder's
over-looking, and Hareton with all his bashfulness isn't
a model of nice behaviour. I let him know that his cousin
would very likely sit with us, and she had been always
used to see the Sabbath respected, so he had as good leave
his guns, and bits of indoor work alone, while she stayed.

'He coloured up at the news; and cast his eyes over his
hands and clothes. The trainoil and gunpowder were
shoved out of sight in a minute. I saw he meant to give
her his company; and I guessed, by his way, he wanted
to be presentable; so, laughing, as I durst not laugh when
the master is by, I offered to help him, if he would, and
joked at his confusion. He grew sullen, and began to
swear.

'Now, Mrs. Dean,' she went on, seeing me not pleased
by her manner, 'you happen think your young lady too
fine for Mr. Hareton, and happen you're right—but, I own,
72

I should love well to bring her pride a peg lower. And what will all her learning and her daintiness do for her, now? She's as poor as you, or I—poorer—I'll be bound, you're saying—and I'm doing my little all, that road.'

Hareton allowed Zillah to give him her aid; and she flattered him into a good humour; so, when Catherine came, half forgetting her former insults, he tried to make himself agreeable, by the housekeeper's account.

'Missis walked in,' she said, 'as chill as an icicle, and as high as a princess. I got up and offered her my seat in the armchair. No, she turned up her nose at my civility. Earnshaw rose too, and bid her come to the settle, and sit close by the fire; he was sure she was starved[3].

' "I've been starved a month and more," she answered, resting on the word, as scornful as she could.

'And she got a chair for herself, and placed it at a distance from both of us.

'Having sat till she was warm, she began to look round, and discovered a number of books in the dresser; she was instantly upon her feet again, stretching to reach them, but they were too high up.

'Her cousin, after watching her endeavours a while, at last summoned courage to help her; she held her frock, and he filled it with the first that came to hand.

'That was a great advance for the lad—she didn't thank him; still, he felt gratified that she had accepted his assistance, and ventured to stand behind as she examined them, and even to stoop and point out what struck his fancy in certain old pictures which they contained—nor was he daunted by the saucy style in which she jerked the page from his finger; he contented himself with going a bit farther back, and looking at her, instead of the book.

'She continued reading, or seeking for something to read. His attention became, by degrees, quite centred in the study of her thick, silky curls—her face he couldn't see, and she couldn't see him. And, perhaps, not quite awake to what he did, but attracted like a child to a candle, at last, he proceeded from staring to touching; he put out his hand and stroked one curl, as gently as if it were a bird. He might have stuck a knife into her neck, she started round in such a taking.

'"Get away, this moment! How dare you touch me? Why are you stopping there?" she cried, in a tone of disgust. "I can't endure you! I'll go upstairs again, if you come near me."

'Mr. Hareton recoiled, looking as foolish as he could do; he sat down in the settle, very quiet, and she continued turning over her volumes, another half hour—finally, Earnshaw crossed over, and whispered to me.

'"Will you ask her to read to us, Zillah? I'm stalled[4] of doing naught—and I do like—I could like to hear her! dunnot say I wanted it, but ask of yourseln."

'"Mr. Hareton wishes you would read to us, ma'am," I said, immediately. "He'd take it very kind—he'd be much obliged."

'She frowned; and, looking up, answered,

'"Mr. Hareton, and the whole set of you will be good enough to understand that I reject any pretence at kindness you have the hypocrisy to offer! I despise you, and will have nothing to say to any of you! When I would have given my life for one kind word, even to see one of your faces, you all kept off. But I won't complain to you! I'm driven down here by the cold, not either to amuse you, or enjoy your society."

'"What could I ha' done?" began Earnshaw. "How was I to blame?"

'"Oh! you are an exception," answered Mrs. Heathcliff. "I never missed such a concern as you."

'"But, I offered more than once, and asked," he said,

74

kindling up at her pertness, "I asked Mr. Heathcliff to let me wake for you—"

' "Be silent! I'll go out of doors, or anywhere, rather than have your disagreeable voice in my ear!" said my lady.

'Hareton muttered, she might go to hell, for him! and unslinging his gun, restrained himself from his Sunday occupations, no longer.

Wuthering Heights, ch. 30

*

This is Lockwood's third visit to the Heights, two or three months later than extract 4, but still during his earlier stay in the district—i.e., in January, not the later September visit of extract 1. He speaks.

12

I approached her, pretending to desire a view of the garden; and, as I fancied, adroitly dropped Mrs. Dean's note onto her knee, unnoticed by Hareton—but she asked aloud—

'What is that?' And chucked it off.

'A letter from your old acquaintance, the housekeeper at the Grange,' I answered, annoyed at her exposing my kind deed, and fearful lest it should be imagined a missive of my own.

She would gladly have gathered it up, at this information, but Hareton beat her; he seized, and put it in his waistcoat, saying Mr. Heathcliff should look at it first.

Thereat, Catherine silently turned her face from us, and, very stealthily, drew out her pocket-handkerchief and applied it to her eyes; and her cousin, after struggling a while to keep down his softer feelings, pulled out the letter and flung it on the floor beside her as ungraciously as he could.

Catherine caught, and perused it eagerly; then she put a few questions to me concerning the inmates, rational and irrational, of her former home; and gazing towards the hills, murmured in soliloquy.

'I should like to be riding Minny down there! I should like to be climbing up there—Oh! I'm tired—I'm *stalled*, Hareton!'

And she leant her pretty head back against the sill, with half a yawn and half a sigh, and lapsed into an aspect of abstracted sadness, neither caring nor knowing whether we remarked her.

'Mrs. Heathcliff,' I said, after sitting some time mute, 'you are not aware that I am an acquaintance of yours? so intimate, that I think it strange that you won't come and speak to me. My housekeeper never wearies of talking about and praising you; and she'll be greatly disappointed if I return with no news of, or from you, except that you received her letter and said nothing!'

She appeared to wonder at this speech and asked,

'Does Ellen like you?'

'Yes, very well,' I replied unhesitatingly.

'You must tell her,' she continued, 'that I would answer her letter, but I have no materials for writing, not even a book from which I might tear a leaf.'

'No books!' I exclaimed. 'How do you contrive to live here without them? if I may take the liberty to inquire— Though provided with a large library, I'm frequently very dull at the Grange—take my books away, and I should be desperate!'

Wuthering Heights, ch. 31

Notes
¹ *Catherine*: the elder.
² *Kirk*: the Anglican church, as distinct from the Nonconformist 'chapel'.
³ *starved*: of cold; frozen.
⁴ *stalled*: bored.

In the first of these extracts, perhaps the most interesting matter from the point of view of this section is the function of Heathcliff's speech, which displays several of the uses of conversation mentioned in the headnote. 11 and 12, on the other hand, are chosen to illustrate the varieties of speech among characters. Distinguish these in their dialect, formality, naturalness, and show what the author means by these distinctions and what she uses them for. In particular, note how the word *stalled* is used in 11, and then again in 12, for a particular purpose. (In the novel, the two scenes are close together in succeeding chapters.)

Characterisation in Emily Brontë

In the first of the previous group of extracts, Heath-cliff demonstrates his character by speaking of himself. A more usual mode of characterisation is for the author to come upon people as it were unawares, to show them to the reader in some typical pose or action. The two extracts which follow show how Emily Brontë does this in different ways. In the first we have Heathcliff demonstrating to Nelly how he has the entire family under his thumb. His spoilt and sickly son Linton is made to be friendly with the young Catherine, who is glad of any company of her own age (Heathcliff's plan is to cause a marriage between them, so that he can control the Linton inheritance, which must go to one or the other); and at the same time Heathcliff incites the pair to degrade Hareton, the son of his old enemy Hindley. We therefore see the three contrasted young people together, and in the contrast see their different natures.

But further, the author presents not only what Heath-cliff wants Nelly to see, but also her own view of the situation. The key, unexpectedly, is Hareton, unprivileged and humiliated though he is. Linton's sniggering taunts display his spoilt citified nature better than his physical lassitude, and his sneers at Hareton's 'frightful Yorkshire pronunciation' display him as a would-be dandy, conceited in his southern drawing-room airs and despising Emily Brontë's beloved North-country. Catherine's own sprightliness is in danger of developing likewise into superciliousness, and this, like Hareton's ignorance, must be outgrown before the end. And then Heathcliff's claim to have 'outmatched Hindley' is proved false.

Catherine speaks.

13

'I'll not come here, then; [Linton] shall come to the Grange.'

'It will be too far for me,' murmured her cousin, 'to walk four miles would kill me. No, come here, Miss Catherine, now and then, not every morning, but once or twice a week.'

The father launched towards his son a glance of bitter contempt.

'I am afraid, Nelly, I shall lose my labour,' he muttered to me. 'Miss Catherine, as the ninny calls her, will discover his value, and send him to the devil. Now, if it had been Hareton—do you know that, twenty times a day, I covet Hareton, with all his degradation? I'd have loved the lad had he been some one else. But I think he's safe from *her* love. I'll pit him against that paltry creature, unless it bestir itself briskly. We calculate it will scarcely last till it is eighteen[1]. Oh, confound the vapid thing. He's absorbed in drying his feet, and never looks at her— Linton!'

'Yes, father,' answered the boy.

'Have you nothing to show your cousin, anywhere about; not even a rabbit, or a weasel's nest? Take her into the garden, before you change your shoes; and into the stable to see your horse.'

'Wouldn't you rather sit here?' asked Linton, addressing Cathy in a tone which expressed reluctance to move again.

'I don't know,' she replied, casting a longing look to the door, and evidently eager to be active.

He kept his seat, and shrank closer to the fire.

Heathcliff rose, and went into the kitchen, and from thence to the yard, calling out for Hareton.

Hareton responded, and presently the two re-entered. The young man had been washing himself, as was visible by the glow on his cheeks, and his wetted hair.

'Oh, I'll ask *you*, uncle,' cried Miss Cathy, recollecting the housekeeper's assertion. 'That's not my cousin, is he?'

'Yes,' he replied, 'your mother's nephew. Don't you like him?'

Catherine looked queer.

'Is he not a handsome lad?' he continued.

The uncivil little thing stood on tiptoe, and whispered a sentence in Heathcliff's ear.

He laughed; Hareton darkened; I perceived he was very sensitive to suspected slights, and had obviously a dim notion of his inferiority. But his master or guardian chased the frown by exclaiming—

'You'll be the favourite among us, Hareton! She says you are a—what was it? Well, something very flattering —Here! you go with her round the farm. And behave like a gentleman, mind! Don't use any bad words; and don't stare, when the young lady is not looking at you, and be ready to hide your face when she is; and, when you speak, say your words slowly, and keep your hands out of your pockets. Be off, and entertain her as nicely as you can.'

He watched the couple walking past the window. Earnshaw had his countenance completely averted from his companion. He seemed studying the familiar landscape with a stranger's, and an artist's interest.

Catherine took a sly look at him, expressing small admiration. She then turned her attention to seeking out objects of amusement for herself, and tripped merrily on, lilting a tune to supply the lack of conversation.

'I've tied his tongue,' observed Heathcliff. 'He'll not venture a single syllable, all the time! Nelly, you recollect me at his age—nay, some years younger—Did I ever look so stupid, so "gaumless," as Joseph calls it?'

'Worse,' I replied, 'because more sullen with it.'

'I've a pleasure in him!' he continued reflecting aloud. 'He has satisfied my expectations—if he were a born fool I should not enjoy it half so much—But he's no fool; and I can sympathise with all his feelings, having felt them myself—I know what he suffers now, for instance, exactly —it is merely a beginning of what he shall suffer, though. And he'll never be able to emerge from his bathos of coarseness, and ignorance. I've got him faster than his scoundrel of a father secured me, and lower; for he takes a pride in his brutishness. I've taught him to scorn everything, extra-animal, as silly and weak—Don't you think Hindley would be proud of his son, if he could see him? almost as proud as I am of mine—But there's this difference, one is gold put to the use of paving stones; and the other is tin polished to ape a service of silver—*Mine* has nothing valuable about it; yet I shall have the merit, of making it go as far as such poor stuff can go. *His* had first-rate qualities, and they are lost—rendered worse than unavailing—I have nothing to regret; he would have more than any, but I, are aware of—And the best of it is, Hareton is damnably fond of me! You'll own that I've outmatched Hindley there—If the dead villain could rise from his grave to abuse me for his offspring's wrongs, I should have the fun of seeing the said offspring fight him back again, indignant that he should dare to rail at the one friend he has in the world!'

Heathcliff chuckled a fiendish laugh at the idea; I made no reply, because I saw that he expected none.

Meantime, our young companion, who sat too removed from us to hear what was said, began to evince symptoms of uneasiness: probably repenting that he had denied himself the treat of Catherine's society, for fear of a little fatigue.

His father remarked the restless glances wandering to the window, and the hand irresolutely extended towards his cap.

'Get up, you idle boy!' he exclaimed with assumed heartiness. 'Away after them . . . they are just at the corner, by the stand of hives.'

Linton gathered his energies, and left the hearth. The lattice was open and, as he stepped out, I heard Cathy inquiring of her unsociable attendant, what was that inscription[2] over the door?

Hareton stared up, and scratched his head like a true clown.

'It's some damnable writing,' he answered. 'I cannot read it.'

'Can't read it?' cried Catherine. 'I can read it . . It's English . . . but I want to know, why it's there.'

Linton giggled—the first appearance of mirth he had exhibited.

'He does not know his letters,' he said to his cousin. 'Could you believe in the existence of such a colossal dunce?'

'Is he all as he should be?' asked Miss Cathy seriously, 'or is he simple . . . not right? I've questioned him twice now, and each time he looked so stupid, I think he does not understand me; I can hardly understand *him*, I'm sure!'

Linton repeated his laugh, and glanced at Hareton taunt- ingly, who certainly did not seem quite clear of compre- hension at that moment.

'There's nothing the matter, but laziness, is there, Earn- shaw?' he said. 'My cousin fancies you are an idiot . . . There you experience the consequence of scorning "book- larning." as you would say . . . Have you noticed, Catherine, his frightful Yorkshire pronunciation?'

'Why, where the devil is the use on 't?' growled Hare- ton, more ready in answering his daily companion. He was about to enlarge further, but the two youngsters broke into a noisy fit of merriment; my giddy Miss being de- lighted to discover that she might turn his strange talk to matter of amusement.

'Where is the use of the devil in that sentence?' tittered Linton. 'Papa told you not to say any bad words, and you can't open your mouth without one . . . Do try to be- have like a gentleman, now do!'

'If thou wern't more a lass than a lad, I'd fell thee this minute, I would; pitiful lath of a crater!' retorted the angry boor retreating, while his face burnt with mingled rage, and mortification; for he was conscious of being in- sulted, and embarrassed how to resent it.

Wuthering Heights, ch. 21

Notes
  [1] Linton is already visibly consumptive.
  [2] Inscription : this reads *Hareton Earnshaw 1500*.

Critics commonly assess an author's characterisations by standards of realism and plausibility, and it is important for any reader at some stage to stop and ask what characterisation is for. It is not an end in itself; a story composed of perfectly plausible characters can make a very lifeless novel. Emily Brontë's characters are often larger than life; a study of earlier extracts in comparison with nos. 13 and 15 will show that character, like motion, scenery, imagery and comment, is only a part of the total pattern of understanding of human life which the novel contains. One might take as a basis for discussion the headnote's remark that 'the key . . . is Hareton'. Besides discussing the purpose of characterisation, the student should note that speech is not the only way of displaying it, and should see what other means are used besides.

Characterisation in Anne Brontë

The Tenant of Wildfell Hall offers an interesting piece of
half-ironic characterisation. The heroine, Helen Huntingdon, is a woman who is much offended against by her husband, and she stands as a true heroine, a virtuous figure
against his callousness. This would be very acceptable to
the reader, in spite of the objections to the book (which
were referred to in the previous section, 9). But there is
more to Anne's writing than that; for she also hints in her
portrayal that 'virtue', in the sense of conscious rectitude,
is not enough. Helen is inclined to be 'unco' guid'; her
virtue is that of the genteel lady, too rigid and pedantic to
be attractive. Her husband is undoubtedly a useless and
selfish person, but her attitude could hardly improve him,
or endear her to him. Anne Brontë makes only rare comments on this—sufficient to make it clear that this was
the effect intended—and otherwise leaves her character
to display itself.

In the following passage, she finds herself in the company of Lady Lowborough who, she has come to realise, is
her husband's mistress. Mr. Hargrave, also realising this,
has offered love to her, and she has indignantly refused
him.

14

In the course of the morning, I drove over to the Grove with the two ladies, to give Milicent an opportunity for bidding farewell to her mother and sister. They persuaded her to stay with them the rest of the day, Mrs. Hargrave promising to bring her back in the evening and remain till the party broke up on the morrow. Consequently, Lady Lowborough and I had the pleasure of returning *tête-à-tête* in the carriage together. For the first mile or two, we kept silence, I looking out of my window, and she leaning back in her corner. But I was not going to restrict myself to any particular position for her: when I was tired of leaning forward, with the cold, raw wind in my face, and surveying the russet hedges, and the damp, tangled grass of their banks, I gave it up, and leant back too. With her usual impudence, my companion then made some attempts to get up a conversation; but the monosyllables 'yes,' or 'no,' or 'humph,' were the utmost her several remarks could elicit from me. At last, on her asking my opinion upon some immaterial point of discussion, I answered,—

'Why do you wish to talk to me, Lady Lowborough?—you must know what I think of you.'

'Well, if you will be so bitter against me,' replied she, 'I can't help it;—but I'm not going to sulk for anybody.'

Our short drive was now at an end. As soon as the carriage door was opened she sprang out, and went down the park to meet the gentlemen, who were just returning from the woods. Of course I did not follow.

But I had not done with her impudence yet:—after dinner, I retired to the drawing-room, as usual, and she accompanied me, but I had the two children with me, and I gave them my whole attention, and determined to keep them till the gentlemen came, or till Milicent arrived with her mother. Little Helen, however, was soon tired of playing, and insisted upon going to sleep; and while I sat on the sofa with her on my knee, and Arthur seated beside me, gently playing with her soft flaxen hair,—Lady Lowborough composedly came and placed herself on the other side.

'To-morrow, Mrs. Huntingdon,' said she, 'you will be delivered from my presence, which, no doubt, you will be very glad of—it is natural you should:—but do you know I have rendered you a great service? Shall I tell you what it is?'

'I shall be glad to hear of any service you have rendered me,' said I, determined to be calm, for I knew by the tone of her voice she wanted to provoke me.

'Well,' resumed she, 'have you not observed the salutary change in Mr. Huntingdon? Don't you see what a sober, temperate man he is become? You saw with regret the sad habits he was contracting, I know; and I know you did your utmost to deliver him from them,—but without success, until I came to your assistance. I told him in a few words that I could not bear to see him degrade himself so, and that I should cease to—no matter what I told him, —but you see the reformation I have wrought; and you ought to thank me for it.'

I rose, and rang for the nurse.

'But I desire no thanks,' she continued; 'all the return I ask is, that you will take care of him when I am gone, and not, by harshness and neglect, drive him back to his old courses.'

I was almost sick with passion, but Rachel was now at the door: I pointed to the children, for I could not trust myself to speak: she took them away, and I followed.

'Will you, Helen?' continued the speaker.

I gave her a look that blighted the malicious smile on her face—or checked it, at least for a moment—and departed.

In the ante-room I met Mr. Hargrave. He saw I was in no humour to be spoken to, and suffered me to pass without a word; but when, after a few minutes' seclusion in the library, I had regained my composure, and was returning, to join Mrs. Hargrave and Milicent, whom I had just heard come downstairs and go into the drawing-room, I found him there still, lingering in the dimly-lighted apartment, and evidently waiting for me.

'Mrs. Huntingdon,' said he, as I passed, 'will you allow me one word?'

'What is it, then?—be quick, if you please.'

'I offended you this morning; and I cannot live under your displeasure.'

'Then, go, and sin no more,' replied I, turning away.

'No, no!' said he, hastily, setting himself before me— 'Pardon me, but I must have your forgiveness. I leave you to-morrow, and I may not have an opportunity of speaking to you again. I was wrong to forget myself—and you, as I did; but let me implore you to forget and forgive my rash presumption, and think of me as if those words had never been spoken; for, believe me, I regret them deeply, and the loss of your esteem is too severe a penalty—I cannot bear it.'

'Forgetfulness is not to be purchased with a wish; and I cannot bestow my esteem on all who desire it, unless they deserve it too.'

'I shall think my life well spent in labouring to deserve it, if you will but pardon this offence—Will you?'

'Yes.'

'Yes! but that is coldly spoken. Give me your hand and I'll believe you. You won't? Then, Mrs. Huntingdon, you do not forgive me!'

'Yes—here it is, and my forgiveness with it: only—*sin no more.*'

He pressed my cold hand with sentimental fervour, but

said nothing, and stood aside to let me pass into the room, where all the company were now assembled. Mr. Grimsby was seated near the door: on seeing me enter, almost immediately followed by Hargrave, he leered at me, with a glance of intolerable significance, as I passed. I looked him in the face, till he sullenly turned away, if not ashamed, at least confounded for the moment. Meantime, Hattersley had seized Hargrave by the arm, and was whispering something in his ear—some coarse joke, no doubt, for the latter neither laughed nor spoke in answer, but, turning from him with a slight curl of the lip, disengaged himself and went to his mother, who was telling Lord Lowborough how many reasons she had to be proud of her son.

Thank Heaven, they are all going to-morrow.

The Tenant of Wildfell Hall, ch. 35

There are two ways of looking at Helen Huntingdon as she appears in this passage. The first is simply to consider how it brings out her character—which it does by reflection quite as much as by direct presentation. The second is to see how the author, through the same indirect process, also manages to convey her attitude to Helen. The 'correctness' of social observance, in particular, is skilfully used to point both character and atmosphere. But note the greater simplicity of Anne's style in comparison with Emily's. Anne makes much less use of the detailed implications which can be drawn from small circumstances, such as the black-and-white shading in Heathcliff's appearance in extract 7. (That is a case of symbolism, the mystery of the man's character as a whole being pointed by the otherwise irrelevant effect of moonlight as he stands at the gate. But *symbolism* is a much-misused word, to be handled with care.)

Characterisation in Emily Brontë

This extract is an example of a more prolonged and deliberate piece of characterisation; the author wants to establish the kind of person Cathy had become as she grew into a woman. Here the point is made first by her own behaviour, and second by a series of contrasts with other natures—Heathcliff, Nelly, Edgar (here scarcely more than children). Nelly is an 'ordinary person', and as such is the measure of Cathy's waywardness. Edgar Linton is partly a contrast, being quiet and polite to the extent of weakness; and partly a foil, being easily bent to Cathy's whim.

Characterisation is not an end in itself, but a part of the plot. This scene displays Cathy as she always will be, and sets in motion one of the most important series of events in the novel, leading through her perverse marriage to Edgar towards Heathcliff's retaliation and to her death, which does not end her power over Heathcliff.

15

'And should I always be sitting with you?' she demanded, growing more irritated. 'What good do I get—what do you talk about? you might be dumb or a baby for anything you say to amuse me, or for anything you do, either!'

'You never told me, before, that I talked too little, or that you disliked my company, Cathy!' exclaimed Heathcliff in much agitation.

'It's no company at all, when people know nothing and say nothing,' she muttered.

Her companion rose up, but he hadn't time to express his feelings further, for a horse's feet were heard on the flags, and, having knocked gently, young Linton entered, his face brilliant with delight at the unexpected summons he had received.

Doubtless Catherine marked the difference between her friends as one came in, and the other went out. The contrast resembled what you see in exchanging a bleak, hilly, coal country, for a beautiful fertile valley; and his voice and greeting were as opposite as his aspect—He had a sweet, low manner of speaking, and pronounced his words as you do, that's less gruff than we talk here and softer.

'I'm not come too soon, am I?' he said, casting a look at me; I had begun to wipe the plate, and tidy some drawers at the far end in the dresser.

'No,' answered Catherine. 'What are you doing there, Nelly?'

'My work, Miss,' I replied. (Mr. Hindley had given me directions to make a third party in any private visits Linton chose to pay.)

She stepped behind me and whispered crossly, 'Take yourself and your dusters off! when company are in the house, servants don't commence scouring and cleaning in the room where they are!'

'It's a good opportunity, now that master is away,' I
you say to amuse me, or for anything you do, either!'
things in his presence—I'm sure Mr. Edgar will excuse me.'

'I hate you to be fidgeting in *my* presence,' exclaimed

the young lady imperiously, not allowing her guest time to speak—she had failed to recover her equanimity since the little dispute with Heathcliff.

'I'm sorry for it, Miss Catherine!' was my response; and I proceeded assiduously with my occupation.

She, supposing Edgar could not see her, snatched the cloth from my hand, and pinched me, with a prolonged wrench, very spitefully on the arm.

I've said I did not love her; and rather relished mortifying her vanity, now and then; besides, she hurt me extremely, so I started up from my knees, and screamed out,

'Oh, Miss, that's a nasty trick! You have no right to nip me, and I'm not going to bear it!'

'I didn't touch you, you lying creature!' cried she, her fingers tingling to repeat the act, and her ears red with rage. She never had power to conceal her passion, it always set her whole complexion in a blaze.

'What's that, then?' I retorted, showing a decided purple witness to refute her.

She stamped her foot, wavered a moment, and then, irresistibly impelled by the naughty spirit within her, slapped me on the cheek a stinging blow that filled both eyes with water.

'Catherine, love! Catherine!' interposed Linton, greatly shocked at the double fault of falsehood and violence, which his idol had committed.

'Leave the room, Ellen!' she repeated, trembling all over.

Little Hareton, who followed me everywhere, and was sitting near me on the floor, at seeing my tears commenced crying himself, and sobbed out complaints against 'wicked aunt Cathy,' which drew her fury on to his unlucky head: she seized his shoulders, and shook him till the poor child waxed livid, and Edgar thoughtlessly laid hold of her hands to deliver him. In an instant one was wrung free, and the astonished young man felt it applied over his own ear in a way that could not be mistaken for jest.

He drew back in consternation—I lifted Hareton in my arms, and walked off to the kitchen with him; leaving the door of communication open, for I was curious to watch how they would settle their disagreement.

The insulted visitor moved to the spot where he had laid his hat, pale and with a quivering lip.

'That's right!' I said to myself, 'Take warning and be-gone! It's a kindness to let you have a glimpse of her genuine disposition.'

'Where are you going?' demanded Catherine, advancing to the door.

He swerved aside and attempted to pass.

'You must not go!' she exclaimed energetically.

'I must and shall!' he replied in a subdued voice.

'No,' she persisted, grasping the handle; 'not yet, Edgar Linton—sit down, you shall not leave me in that temper. I should be miserable all night, and I won't be miserable for you!'

'Can I stay after you have struck me?' asked Linton.

Catherine was mute.

'You've made me afraid, and ashamed of you,' he continued; 'I'll not come here again!'

Her eyes began to glisten and her lids to twinkle.

'And you told a deliberate untruth!' he said.

'I didn't!' she cried, recovering her speech. 'I did nothing deliberately—Well, go, if you please—get away! And now I'll cry—I'll cry myself sick!'

She dropped down on her knees by a chair and set to weeping in serious earnest.

Edgar persevered in his resolution as far as the court; there he lingered. I resolved to encourage him.

'Miss is dreadfully wayward, sir!' I called out. 'As bad

as any marred child—you'd better be riding home, or else she will be sick, only to grieve us.'

The soft thing looked askance through the window—he possessed the power to depart, as much as a cat possesses the power to leave a mouse half killed, or a bird half eaten—

Ah, I thought; there will be no saving him—He's doomed, and flies to his fate!

And, so it was, he turned abruptly, hastened into the house again, shut the door behind him; and, when I went in a while after to inform them that Earnshaw had come home rabid drunk, ready to pull the old place about our ears (his ordinary frame of mind in that condition) I saw the quarrel had merely effected a closer intimacy— had broken the outworks of youthful timidity, and enabled them to forsake the disguise of friendship, and confess themselves lovers.

Wuthering Heights, ch. 8

Many of the points dealt with in studying the last two extracts may be found again here. But since this passage is particularly important in revealing Cathy's character, it is important to see what kind of character this is. To what extent is it a plausible invention; and what more is it than that? Is it true that her most evident characteristic is selfishness? (But selfishness can take many forms.) What does Emily Brontë think of her? Nelly and Edgar, too, are used here, not so much to reveal themselves as to reveal more about Cathy. Heathcliff's place in the scene, although he leaves it almost at the beginning, is also important, both for the mark which he always leaves behind him, even in childhood, and for the difference between him and both Cathy and Edgar, in different ways.

This passage is also useful as a basis for a study of Emily Brontë's moral attitudes (in distinction with Anne's, shown in extracts 9 and 14). Note how, in this and other extracts (e.g. nos. 1, 7 and 10) Nelly is used as the vehicle of moral opinion. Is Emily therefore to be identified with Nelly's opinions? Nelly has a character of her own; consider how Emily's own opinions filter through this character, and by other ways. What can be determined about Emily Brontë's moral attitudes?

'Agnes Grey'

This extract illustrates many of the features of Anne
Brontë's first novel, *Agnes Grey*. The transparency of her
style is in striking contrast to the subtle allusiveness of
Wuthering Heights. There are no images or suggestions
carrying meaning and purpose from one scene to another.
The irony is plain to see, and so is the gentle moralising
which is characteristic of the book, conveying as it does
a belief in the advantages of common life, as against the
thoughtless thrills of Rosalie Murray's 'society' existence.
In Miss Phyllis Bentley's phrase, Anne's writing is marked
by 'piety and realism'.

In accordance with etiquette, the elder sister Rosalie is
'Miss Murray'; the younger is 'Miss Matilda'. Agnes Grey
is their governess. Rosalie, following her character as
displayed here, marries for show and lives to regret it.
As this extract suggests, the novel is not profound, but
honest, straightforward and pleasant.

16

At eighteen, Miss Murray was to emerge from the quiet
obscurity of the schoolroom into the full blaze of the
fashionable world—as much of it, at least, as could be

had out of London; for her papa could not be persuaded to leave his rural pleasures and pursuits, even for a few weeks' residence in town. She was to make her debut on the third of January, at a magnificent ball, which her mamma proposed to give to all nobility and choice gentry of O—— and its neighbourhood for twenty miles round. Of course, she looked forward to it with the wildest impatience, and the most extravagant anticipations of delight.

'Miss Grey,' said she, one evening, a month before the all-important day, as I was perusing a long and extremely interesting letter of my sister's,—which I had just glanced at in the morning to see that it contained no very bad news, and kept till now, unable before to find a quiet moment for reading it,—'Miss Grey, do put away that dull, stupid letter, and listen to me! I'm sure my talk must be far more amusing than that.'

She seated herself on the low stool at my feet; and I, suppressing a sigh of vexation, began to fold up the epistle.

'You should tell the good people at home not to bore you with such long letters,' said she; 'and above all, do bid them to write on proper notepaper, and not on those great vulgar sheets. You should see the charming little lady-like notes mamma writes to her friends.'

'The good people at home,' replied I, 'know very well that the longer their letters are, the better I like them. I should be very sorry to receive a charming little lady-like note from any of them; and I thought you were too much of a lady yourself, Miss Murray, to talk about the 'vulgarity' of writing on a large sheet of paper.'

'Well, I only said it to tease you. But now I want to talk about the ball; and to tell you that you positively must put off your holidays till it is over.'

'Why so?—I shall not be present at the ball.'

97

'No, but you will see the rooms decked out before it begins, and hear the music, and, above all, see me in my splendid new dress. I shall be so charming, you'll be ready to worship me—you really must stay.'

'I should like to see you very much; but I shall have many opportunities of seeing you equally charming, on the occasion of some of the numberless balls and parties that are to be, and I cannot disappoint my friends by postponing my return so long.'

'Oh, never mind your friends! Tell them we won't let you go.'

'But, to say the truth, it would be a disappointment to myself: I long to see them as much as they to see me—perhaps more.'

'Well, but it is such a short time.'

'Nearly a fortnight by my computation; and, besides, I cannot bear the thoughts of a Christmas spent from home: and, moreover, my sister is going to be married.'

'Is she—when?'

'Not till next month; but I want to be there to assist her in making preparations, and to make the best of her company while we have her.'

'Why didn't you tell me before?'

'I've only got the news in this letter, which you stigmatise as dull and stupid, and won't let me read.'

'To whom is she to be married?'

'To Mr. Richardson, the vicar of a neighbouring parish.'

'Is he rich?'

'No; only comfortable.'

'Is he handsome?'

'No; only decent.'

'Young?'

'No; only middling.'

'Oh stop!—you'll make me sick. How *can* she bear it?'

'A quiet little vicarage, with an ivy-clad porch, an old-fashioned garden, and—'

'Oh stop!—you'll make me sick. How *can* she bear it?'

'I expect she'll not only be able to bear it, but to be very happy. You did not ask me if Mr. Richardson were a good, wise, or amiable man; I could have answered Yes, to all these questions—at least so Mary thinks, and I hope she will not find herself mistaken.'

'But—miserable creature! how can she think of spending her life there, cooped up with that nasty old man; and *no* hope of change?'

'He is not old: he is only six or seven and thirty; and she herself is twenty-eight, and as sober as if she were fifty.'

'Oh! that's better then—they're well matched: but do they call him the "worthy vicar"?'

'I don't know; but if they do, I believe he merits the epithet.'

'Mercy, how shocking! and will she wear a white apron, and make pies and puddings?'

'I don't know about the white apron, but I dare say she will make pies and puddings now and then; but that will be no great hardship, as she has done it before.'

Agnes Grey, ch. 8

This passage has none of the intensity of Emily Brontë's writing. It derives its interest from different sources. Anne Brontë is not trying to stir new depths of feeling in the reader, but to depict and interpret quite ordinary people in a pointed way. Irony and implication are among her means. Her people are realistic; yet, as pointed out in extract 10, realism is only a means to an end—here, to social comment. The social life of the passage is that of a family accustomed, not to the rough practicalities of the Dales, as in *Wuthering Heights*, but to the more sophisticated gentleman-farmer's residence of the Vale of York. Such places did exist, and such young ladies did read novels. Anne Brontë's story, then, had a purpose which Emily's did not, and the romantic view of literature is not the only true one.

Recurrent Imagery in 'Wuthering Heights': the supernatural

The last extract from *Wuthering Heights*, no 17, illustrates many of the points already made, and in addition contains those elements which give a special flavour to this novel. The scene is the Grange, the bedroom of the elder Cathy who has locked herself away in a hysteric outburst, and in three days weakened herself into real illness, which develops into a 'brain fever'. She partially recovers, only to linger on as an invalid, and to die in childbirth. (The limitations of the diagnostic medicine of the period produce such descriptions of disease, unsatisfactory to us, as 'brain fever'—though the diseases were real enough.)

In extracts 6 and 7 there were images of the bedroom at the Heights, its window, bed and press; and of Gimmerton chapel, its graveyard and the beck nearby. Here they recur together, as they repeatedly do in the book, forming a background to a crisis. The effects of the different images vary. Because of Lockwood's dream in chapter 3 the bedroom images are always sinister, while the Gimmerton places are sometimes beautiful, sometimes melancholy; but the purpose of their use is always the same. *Wuthering Heights* is one of the few novels which may justifiably be called 'poetic'; that is, its meaning is attained not only by the writer's control of elements that can be analysed and explained logically, such as plot, character, argument, judgements and the like. It is also reached through the hidden emotional forces of imagery, and the accumulation of feeling through all forms of perception at once. These images, simple in themselves, and often repeated, give the reader a sense of wholeness and unity, and at the same time of inevitability—wherever he turns he comes back to the same places. This effect is not achieved by rational calculation—rationally these images have no special meaning—but imaginatively.

Secondly, this extract illustrates Emily Brontë's use of the 'supernatural'. Her achievement is to exploit successfully the reader's well-established liking for the marvellous and the uncanny, while never giving his modern mind an opportunity to say 'This is impossible'. There are no impossibilities in *Wuthering Heights*. Yet at times the characters act as if living in a magic world. Nelly insists that the strangeness of Cathy's words is caused by her illness: nevertheless, the reader cannot avoid seeing that what Cathy foretells so wildly comes true. Heathcliff continues to 'follow' her; we have seen how Lockwood dreams of her at the window of the Heights; the book ends with him standing by Gimmerton kirk over the graves of Edgar, Cathy and Heathcliff. Other correspondences will be seen as the book is read through. The novel is 'plausible' not because it makes physical and psychological probability, but because it satisfies the instinct for wholeness, a unified view and shape of the little world of the story.

The scene is the bedroom at Thrushcross Grange: the *she* of the first line is Cathy.

17

A minute previously she was violent; now, supported on one arm, and not noticing my refusal to obey her, she seemed to find childish diversion in pulling the feathers from the rents she had just made, and ranging them on the sheet according to their different species: her mind had strayed to other associations.

'That's a turkey's,' she murmured to herself; 'and this is a wild duck's; and this is a pigeon's. Ah, they put pigeons' feathers in the pillows—no wonder I couldn't die! Let me take care to throw it on the floor when I lie down. And here's a moor-cock's; and this—I should know it among a thousand—it's a lapwing's. Bonny bird; wheeling over our heads in the middle of the moor. It wanted to get to its nest, for the clouds touched the swells, and it felt rain coming. This feather was picked up from the heath, the bird was not shot—we saw its nest in the winter, full of little skeletons. Heathcliff set a trap over it, and the old ones dare not come. I made him promise he'd never shoot a lapwing, after that, and he didn't. Yes, here are more! Did he shoot my lapwings, Nelly? Are they red, any of them? Let me look.'

'Give over with that baby-work!' I interrupted, dragging the pillow away, and turning the holes towards the mattress, for she was removing its contents by handfuls. 'Lie down and shut your eyes, you're wandering. There's a mess! The down is flying about like snow!'

I went here and there collecting it.

'I see in you, Nelly,' she continued, dreamily, 'an aged woman—you have grey hair, and bent shoulders. This bed is the fairy cave under Penistone Crag, and you are gathering elf-bolts to hurt our heifers; pretending, while I am near, that they are only locks of wool. That's what you'll come to fifty years hence: I know you are not so

103

now. I'm not wandering, you're mistaken, or else I should believe you really *were* that withered hag, and I should think I *was* under Penistone Crag, and I'm conscious it's night, and there are two candles on the table making the black press shine like jet.'

'The black press? where is that?' I asked. 'You are talking in your sleep!'

'It's against the wall, as it always is,' she replied. 'It *does* appear odd—I see a face in it!'

'There is no press[1] in the room, and never was,' said I, resuming my seat, and looping up the curtain that I might watch her.

'Don't *you* see that face?' she enquired, gazing earnestly at the mirror.

And say what I could, I was incapable of making her comprehend it to be her own; so I rose and covered it with a shawl.

'It's behind there still!' she pursued, anxiously. 'And it stirred. Who is it? I hope it will not come out when you are gone! Oh! Nelly, the room is haunted! I'm afraid of being alone!'

I took her hand in mine, and bid her to be composed, for a succession of shudders convulsed her frame, and she *would* keep straining her gaze towards the glass.

'There's nobody here!' I insisted. 'It was *yourself*, Mrs. Linton; you knew it a while since.'

'Myself,' she gasped, 'and the clock is striking twelve! It's true, then, that's dreadful!'

Her fingers clutched the clothes, and gathered them over her eyes. I attempted to steal to the door with an intention of calling her husband; but I was summoned back by a piercing shriek. The shawl had dropped from the frame.

'Why, what *is* the matter?' cried I. 'Who is coward now? Wake up! That is the glass—the mirror, Mrs. Linton; and you see yourself in it, and there am I too by your side.'

Trembling and bewildered, she held me fast, but the horror gradually passed from her countenance; its paleness gave place to a glow of shame.

'Oh, dear! I thought I was at home,' she sighed. 'I thought I was lying in my chamber at Wuthering Heights. Because I'm weak, my brain got confused, and I screamed unconsciously. Don't say anything; but stay with me. I dread sleeping, my dreams appal me.'

'A sound sleep would do you good, ma'am,' I answered; 'and I hope this suffering will prevent your trying starving again.'

'Oh, if I were but in my own bed in the old house!' she went on bitterly, wringing her hands. 'And that wind sounding in the firs by the lattice. Do let me feel it—it comes straight down the moor—do let me have one breath!'

To pacify her, I held the casement ajar, a few seconds. A cold blast rushed through, I closed it, and returned to my post.

She lay still now, her face bathed in tears—Exhaustion of body had entirely subdued her spirit; our fiery Catherine was no better than a wailing child!

'How long is it since I shut myself in here?' she asked, suddenly reviving.

'It was Monday evening,' I replied, 'and this is Thursday night, or rather Friday morning, at present.'

'What! of the same week?' she exclaimed. 'Only that brief time?'

'Long enough to live on nothing but cold water, and ill-temper,' observed I.

'Well, it seems a weary number of hours,' she muttered doubtfully, 'it must be more—I remember being in the parlour, after they had quarrelled; and Edgar being cruelly

provoking, and me running into this room desperate—
As soon as ever I had barred the door, utter blackness
overwhelmed me, and I fell on the floor—I couldn't
explain to Edgar how certain I felt of having a fit, or going
raging mad, if he persisted in teasing me! I had no com-
mand of tongue, or brain, and he did not guess my agony,
perhaps; it barely left me sense to try to escape from him
and his voice—Before I recovered sufficiently to see and
hear, it began to be dawn; and Nelly, I'll tell you what I
thought, and what has kept recurring and recurring till I
feared for my reason—I thought as I lay there with my
head against that table leg, and my eyes dimly discerning
the grey square of the window, that I was enclosed in the
oak-panelled bed at home; and my heart ached with some
great grief which, just waking, I could not recollect—I
pondered, and worried myself to discover what it could
be; and most strangely, the whole last seven years of my
life grew a blank! I did not recall that they had been at
all. I was a child; my father was just buried, and my
misery arose from the separation that Hindley had ordered
between me, and Heathcliff—I was laid alone, for the first
time, and rousing from a dismal dose after a night of weeping—I lifted my hand to push the panels aside, it struck
the tabletop! I swept it along the carpet, and then,
memory burst in—my late anguish was swallowed in a
paroxysm of despair—I cannot say why I felt so wildly
wretched—it must have been temporary derangement for
there is scarcely cause—But, supposing at twelve years
old, I had been wrenched from the Heights, and every early
association, and my all in all, as Heathcliff was at that
time, and been converted, at a stroke, into Mrs. Linton,
the lady of Thrushcross Grange, and the wife of a stranger;
an exile, and outcast, thenceforth, from what had been my
world—You may fancy a glimpse of the abyss where I
grovelled! Shake your head as you will, Nelly, *you* have

helped to unsettle me! You should have spoken to Edgar, indeed you should, and compelled him to leave me quiet! Oh, I'm burning! I wish I were out of doors—I wish I were a girl again, half savage and hardy, and free . . . and laughing at injuries, not maddening under them! Why am I so changed? why does my blood rush into a hell of tumult at a few words? I'm sure I should be myself were I once among the heather on those hills . . . Open the window again wide, fasten it open! Quick, why don't you move?'

'Because, I won't give you your death of cold,' I answered.

'You won't give me a chance of life, you mean,' she said, sullenly. 'However, I'm not helpless yet, I'll open it myself.'

And sliding from the bed before I could hinder her, she crossed the room, walking very uncertainly, threw it back, and bent out, careless of the frosty air that cut about her shoulders as keen as a knife.

I entreated, and finally attempted to force her to retire. But I soon found her delirious strength much surpassed mine; (she *was* delirious, I became convinced by her subsequent actions and ravings).

There was no moon, and everything beneath lay in misty darkness; not a light gleamed from any house, far or near; all had been extinguished long ago; and those at Wuthering Heights were never visible . . . still she asserted she caught their shining.

'Look!' she cried eagerly, 'that's my room, with the candle in it, and the trees swaying before it . . . and the other candle is in Joseph's garret . . . Joseph sits up late, doesn't he? He's waiting till I come home that he may lock the gate . . . Well, he'll wait a while yet. It's a rough journey, and a sad heart to travel it; and we must pass by Gimmerton Kirk, to go that journey! We've braved its ghosts often together, and dared each other to stand among the graves and ask them to come . . . But Heathcliff, if I dare you now, will you venture? If you do, I'll keep you. I'll not lie there by myself; they may bury me twelve feet deep, and throw the church down over me; but I won't rest till you are with me. . . . I never will!'

She paused, and resumed with a strange smile. 'He's considering . . . he'd rather I'd come to him! Find a way, then! not through that Kirkyard . . . You are slow! Be content, you always followed me!'

Perceiving it vain to argue against her insanity, I was planning how I could reach something to wrap about her, without quitting my hold of herself, for I could not trust her alone by the gaping lattice; when to my consternation, I heard the rattle of the door-handle, and Mr. Linton entered.

Wuthering Heights, ch. 12

Note
  [1] 'There is no press . . .': See extract 6, headnote; the press is part of the furniture of Cathy's childhood bedroom at the Heights.

The subject of this extract obviously covers far more than the extract itself. Read again the previous extracts, to see how often, and in what circumstances, images recur. When reading the whole book, keep watch for such recurrences. It is important, too, to consider what effect these images create. For example, take these phrases from this extract: 'The black press shining like jet'; 'that wind sounding in the firs by the lattice': 'we must pass by Gimmerton Kirk . . .' What are these images about— and do they mean the same thing every time they occur?

The structure of 'Wuthering Heights'

No scheme of extracts can do justice to *Wuthering Heights*. This statement would be true of any novel; sampling can only indicate the kind of contents the reader may expect. But *Wuthering Heights* is an example of the kind of novel that only makes its effect by gradual development, by its accumulation of telling detail. Over and over again the reader passes some small matter almost without noticing, only to realise, perhaps several chapters later, the force of this apparently insignificant detail. On the other hand, the tension of a long sequence of events can charge quite simple scenes with greatly increased force, as was shown in the first extract. In the headnotes, attention has been drawn to both these effects. The first is illustrated by the constant reappearance of the press and bed at the Heights, and the second by the sense of relaxation in the household after Heathcliff's death.

But it is possible to go further, and say that the story is so constructed that it cannot be regarded as a mere sequence of events. It is conceived and developed as a whole in which the parts are repeatedly seen to be related to one another. The order in which the story is told is not devised only for the interest which lies in variety. It is devised so as to make the reader see, from the very beginning, the shape of the whole. Lockwood arrives at Wuthering Heights in chapter 1 just as Heathcliff is beginning to enjoy the satisfaction of completing his many years' revenge: Catherine and Hareton are in his power, and at odds with one another; their inheritances are his also. Yet —and this is an equal half of the picture—he is not satisfied, because he is still haunted by his longing for his dead sweetheart Cathy. Most of the rest of the book is filled with Nelly's narrative of how this situation came about; finally there is an epilogue, the return of Lockwood and his discovery that the situation has resolved itself. Heathcliff has died in a dream of Cathy, his two victims are restored and reconciled, and the whole nightmare is evaporated in the last lines of the book. Thus the novel is made up of three parts; a prologue, the main narrative, and an epilogue; and the parts are designed to fit together. Chronological sequence is less important than imaginative association.

So with the entire book. As a bare narrative, the story would be highly implausible, with a distinct tendency to melodrama. The inability of anyone to defeat Heathcliff's purpose, the wildness of his behaviour and of his passion for Cathy, the illegality of his hold over the two houses, would all make the reader reject the plot as implausible, were it not for the imaginative power with which Emily Brontë develops her themes. The novel has the plausibility of myth. That is to say, it is plausible not because one can say, 'This might really have happened, in Yorkshire, between 1775 and 1801', but because one can say, 'If it could have happened, this is how it would have been; this is what it would have looked like.' A novel, as much as a play or a poem, is a work of art. It does not satisfy by being 'true to life', but by being true to the imagination.

Exercises

(These are designed to be carried out after the whole book has been read.)

1. On reading the book a second time, note: (a) the way in which the chronological order is rearranged; (b) what incidents are selected by the author for full treatment, out of the many that make up the whole story, and the relative importance she gives them; (c) the use of minor details (e.g. the boundary-stone in ch. 11) which illuminate the narrative; (d) any other methods by which she throws light on the meaning of incidents or actions.

2. How are the characters of the following developed:
    Cathy; Lockwood; Catherine?

3. Assemble evidence of the activity of images (see extract 17).

4. 'Why did I think of *Linton?*' (extract 6, page 43). Lockwood is right about this, and about the 'twenty years', though he knows nothing of the situation. Why does Emily Brontë do this?

Select bibliography

The Works of Emily Brontë

Poems, ed. C. W. Hatfield, Columbia University Press, New York; Oxford University Press, London, 1941. The standard complete edition.

Wuthering Heights (1847). There are many editions of this novel in print; a large number follow the text of the second edition of 1850. The following is a selection, not a comprehensive list. Beware abridged editions.

    a. ed. D. Daiches, Penguin Books, London and New York, 1965

    b. ed. M. Lane, Everyman's Library, Dent, London; E. P. Dutton, New York, 1964. Also includes the poems.

    c. ed. H. W. Garrod, World's Classics, Oxford University Press, London and New York, 1930

    d. ed. M. Schorer, Holt, Rinehart and Wilson, New York, 1950

    e. ed. V. S. Pritchett, Riverside edition, Houghton Mifflin, New York, 1965

    f. ed. T. Crehan, University of London Press, London, 1962

g. ed. W. M. Sale, Norton, New York, 1965. Authoritative text with essays in criticism.

h. ed. J. W. Johnson, Houghton Mifflin, New York, 1966. With suggestions for reading and criticism.

i. with *Selected Poems*. Pan Books, London, 1967

The Works of Anne Brontë

Complete Poems of Anne Brontë, ed. C. Shorter, bibliographical introduction by C. W. Hatfield, Hodder & Stoughton, London, 1923. Shorter is not a very reliable critic, but Hatfield is a sound textual editor.

Agnes Grey (1847)

a. World's Classics, Oxford University Press, London and New York, 1954

b. with *The Tenant of Wildfell Hall*, ed. P. Bentley, New Classics Series, Collins, London and New York, 1954

c. First Novel Library Series (paperback), Cassell, London, 1966

The Tenant of Wildfell Hall (1848)

a. World's Classics Series, Oxford University Press, London and New York, 1907

b. Zodiac Series, Chatto and Windus, London, 1954

c. with *Agnes Grey*, ed. Margaret Lane, Everyman's Library, Dent, London; E. P. Dutton, New York, 1965

d. Harcourt Brace, New York, 1962

Biography and Criticism

BENTLEY, PHYLLIS, *The Brontës*, Arthur Barker, London (2nd edn.), 1966.

The Brontë Sisters, Longmans (for the British Council), London, 1950. A brief but excellent pamphlet. Miss Bentley's works are marked by both local knowledge and good sense.

BLONDEL, J., *Emily Brontë*, Presses Universitaires de France, Paris, 1955. Written in French; mentioned here nevertheless since it is accepted as a most profound study of Emily Brontë and her work. The student should keep it in mind, though it is not to be read by the beginner.

BRONTË, CHARLOTTE, *Shirley* (1849). This is a work of fiction, but the leading character, Shirley, is a picture of Emily as Charlotte saw her. Recommended editions:
    a. ed. P. Bentley, New Classics Series, Collins, London, 1953
    b. ed. M. Lane, Everyman's Library, Dent, London; E. P. Dutton, New York, 1955
    c. World's Classics Series, Oxford University Press, London and New York

CECIL, DAVID, *Early Victorian Novelists*, Fontana Series, Collins, London; University of Chicago, 1964. Chapter on *Wuthering Heights*. A famous interpretation which divides the characters into 'children of the calm' and 'children of the storm', seeing the novel as a conflict between them. This is a great oversimplification, but the essay is illuminating, nevertheless, in many ways.

CHRISTIAN, MILDRED G., in Stevenson, Lionel, *Victorian Fiction, a Guide to Research*, Harvard University Press, 1964. Chapter on the Brontës. This and Moser's book (see below) are useful bibliographical works, up to their dates of publication. This in particular contains, not lists, but a discussion and assessment of the material.

EWBANK, INGA S., *Their Proper Sphere*, Edward Arnold, London, 1966. A study of each of the Brontë sisters in turn, viewing the significance of their situation as women novelists in the mid-nineteenth century.

GASKELL, MRS., *Life of Charlotte Brontë* (1857). This is still the standard biography of the family—not only Charlotte—although it shows some prejudices, particularly against Patrick Brontë.

GOODRIDGE, J. F., *Emily Brontë: Wuthering Heights*, Edward Arnold, London, 1964. A step-by-step examination for the use of students; it has an unfortunate tendency to polysyllablism, but is very sensible in the handling of the subject.

HARRISON, ADA, and STANFORD, DEREK, *Anne Brontë: Her Life and Work*, Methuen, London, 1959. The most balanced biography of Anne.

HOPKINS, ANNETTE B., *The Father of the Brontës*, Johns Hopkins Press, Baltimore, 1958. A very adequate biography of Patrick Brontë, of reasonable length.

LANE, MARGARET, *The Brontë Story: a Reconsideration of Mrs. Gaskell's 'Life of Charlotte Brontë'*, Heinemann, London, 1953. A sound corrective to the faults of Mrs. Gaskell's book, with which it should be read.

MOSER, T. C., *Wuthering Heights—Text, Sources, Criticism*, Harcourt Brace, New York, 1962. See Christian, Mildred G., above.

RATCHFORD, FANNIE E., *The Brontës' Web of Childhood*, Russell, New York, 1941. The classic study of the Brontë family's creation of imaginary lands, and the writing of stories about them.

Gondal's Queen: a Novel in Verse, Nelson, London; University of Texas, 1955. A reconstruction of Emily's tale of Gondal, using the poems as a basis. The reconstruction is necessarily conjectural, but reasonable and illuminating.

RAYMOND, E., *In the Steps of the Brontës*, Rich & Cowan, London, 1948. Primarily written for devotees, who would wish to find the places which the Brontë sisters had incorporated into their novels; but valuable for students who wish to study their handling of actual places and their conversion into fiction.

SANGER, C. P., *The Structure of Wuthering Heights*, Hogarth Press, London, 1926. Although this book is now out of print it is mentioned here because it was a very important essay which demonstrated conclusively that Emily composed *Wuthering Heights* with great care and attention to detail in such practical matters as chronology, family relationships and legal questions. Sanger's main points are summarised in the introduction to Daiches' edition of *Wuthering Heights* and referred to in Goodridge, *Emily Brontë: Wuthering Heights* (see above).

SPARK, MURIEL, *The Brontë Letters*, Nevill, London; University of Oklahoma Press (2nd edn.), 1966. Most of the extant letters are Charlotte's.

SPARK, MURIEL, and STANFORD, DEREK, *Emily Brontë: Her Life and Work*, Peter Owen, London, 1953. Somewhat virulent against other critics at times, but erring on the side of common sense.

TOMPKINS, JOYCE M. S., *Encyclopaedia Britannica* (1967 edn.) article on the Brontës. Informative and critically intelligent, comprehending much material in a little space.

VISICK, MARY, *The Genesis of 'Wuthering Heights'*, Oxford University Press, London and New York, (2nd edn.), 1965. A sympathetic and convincing study of Emily and her book.